On Death and . . . Living!

Memoir of a Soul

by

Michael McCarthy

Clarice,
with all the love
of which we are made,

Michael

Paul Solomon Institute Publications
Virginia Beach, VA
E-MAIL: Psi751@cox.net

Cover design and art by Michael McCarthy
Digital Presentation by Rob Whitehead

With profound gratitude to Aldo Guerreschi for his unselfish sharing of the Shroud of Turin Photo

If you are unable to order this book from your local Bookseller, you may order directly from the publisher.

Email: PSI751@Cox.net
ISBN 978-0-615-53144-1
Printed in the United States of America

I dedicate this book to my beautiful children: Marietta, Michael and Christian.

It is always our children who pay the price for the ignorance we are born into, and the mistakes we make even as we cast off the chains of that ignorance.

I wrote this book so that you too might be able to see how we all have become who we are, while on our way to who we really are.

More beautiful people than you have never walked this earth in any time or place. I love you all, more than you have yet to know ~ but we have forever, and one day we will all "know". And no longer see as through a glass darkly.

Table of Contents

Forward

For Doris:

Thank you, beautiful Soul. See you everywhere...

Death. Easily the most important experience any of us will ever have. Physicists have long acknowledged that the entire physical universe is in a state of "entropy", described in the American Heritage Dictionary as:

"The tendency for all matter and energy in the universe to evolve toward a state of inert uniformity." Sounds like death to me.

So, if everyone and everything everywhere is dying, one might think we would all be seeking diligently to appreciate exactly what that means. Sadly, we grudgingly accept that since we are not yet dead, we cannot truly "know" what death is. By medical definition, death is the absence of bodily functions, sensory experience, and brain activity. The brain-mind, with the enthusiastic support of the "finest minds in their field", understandably accepts that an awareness of *non*-sensory experience is simply unattainable, so we should all just try to keep busy. Keeping busy, by the way, being the very nature of the brain-mind. (More about that during our exciting conclusion.)

But then it gets personal . . .

Far worse than our own demise, because that would immediately give us *all* the answers (though definitely a little late), is the death of someone with whom we have a deep emotional connection, that feeling of oneness with another human being whose simple presence puts a warm happy glow in our life - the very same life that wasn't nearly as much fun until they arrived.

Such love can inspire us to transcend whatever and whoever we thought we were.

Example: You may be just too tired to get up and go to the bathroom to empty your bladder (we are talking real life here). But at that very same moment, you would not hesitate to jump up and head out into a cold dark night to get whatever the object of your affection thinks they need to be happy.

Rejoice! You are profoundly blest! You have found someone who is more important than yourself. If that person should die unexpectedly, you would eagerly trade places with them. It would be an honor, a pleasure, to give your life for theirs.

At this very moment you may be experiencing the loss of someone like that in your life. That may be the reason you are reading this - which brings us to your pain. As anyone who has ever loved can tell you - *real* love causes *real* pain. Indeed, you may still be feeling that burning knife in the center of your chest that makes it difficult to even breathe. What we call 'emotional' pain can obviously be *very* physical.

[*During the process of writing this book, it has been observed by neuro-scientists that the part of the brain activated by physical pain is <u>exactly</u> the same location activated by emotional pain - Love hurts!*]

This is probably not the first time a person you deeply cared for would no longer "be there" for you. In the course of our lives many of those we love will leave us for one reason or another. What makes everything different when they die is, this time there is no talking them out of it. You can't call them up in the middle of the night begging them to come back, or promising to change. This time they are truly and irrevocably gone. Or, at least, so we are told.

Everyone wonders what really takes place when someone dies. We may not talk about it, "comparison shop" our beliefs, so to speak, but even those with no religious or spiritual beliefs at all wonder what will really happen when our life is over. It's just part of being alive.

Example: Suppose someone dies who has done you or someone you care deeply about some serious wrong. Except for those among us already aspiring to sainthood, most of us, even avowed atheists, will at least secretly hope they went somewhere an Honest Universe can return to them exactly what we know they so richly deserve. And, of course, we mean that in a nice way.

Be that as it may, when someone we *love* dies, especially unexpectedly, we are <u>compelled</u> to seek far less ambiguous possibilities. Oh, sure, you may say, "They are in a better place". And that might even suffice for a funeral home conversation. But late at night, when you're all alone? In the darkness of a once familiar place that had only recently been warm and bright, and filled with their love? No. That will <u>not</u> do now.

Now, all of our "deep thoughts" and pontifications - dorm-room, barroom, or barracks philosophy bouts, mystical musings of any and all kinds - are utterly useless. Now, we need to *know!* We need to know that they *are* somewhere, even if we feel we are unable to access that place.

By way of easing our pain, we console each other with phrases alluding to them being "in Heaven"; "on the other side"; "with The Lord"; "over there"; "up there, smiling down on us". Apparently they are everywhere but here.

Well, good news! In almost every case, that is just not true.

Now, for you to actually embrace this fact - and, yes, it is a genuine demonstrable-in-your-own-life fact (or it will be by the time you finish this book) - I'll need to lay down a few *bona fides,* so to speak.

In order for you to embrace and truly understand the rest of this account, you'll first need to accept that I *know* whereof I speak. And, you'll need to know precisely how I came to this understanding (and more importantly, <u>awareness!</u>) so that you can too!

Life is all about <u>experiencing</u>, not just understanding - though a little understanding will take you a very long way, in matters of our true nature. Or, as God-His-Own-Self once asked some old friends of mine:

"Would you seek to study music under a tone deaf psychiatrist, whose wife ran away with the organist?"

Think about it...

On Death and . . Living!

Memoir of a Soul

The Dark Night is Never Expected

I was desperately looking into the eyes of a too young Catholic priest who had, just a few months before, united me in Holy Matrimony with the lifeless body before us. I was praying, begging him, and God, for *any* words that would help me make sense of this nightmare. Words that would have been welcome from anyone, but he was *the* person in that room who was supposed to know about these things.

I was only 20 on the day Doris and I wed, and had, just a few weeks before, turned 21. We celebrated her 18th birthday on July 8th. [Remember that date!]

It was the day after our wedding, and we were still more like kids than real grownups, despite the fact that I was already a graduate of the U. S. Air Force *Air Police School*, and had recently been guarding nuclear-armed aircraft charged with protecting a good portion of the East Coast, including our nation's capitol.

Doris left high school to go to work, to help support her mother and younger sisters. She was the kindest most gentle and loving person I had ever met. And now she was lying in a casket in front of me. To say I was confused and in pain would be an enormous understatement.

I was barely sane, if indeed I was sane at all. I certainly could no longer tell. Still, aside from the fact that I was not even sure I wasn't dreaming this whole thing, I was as calm as anyone could have reasonably hoped. But that was only because my thought processes had completely stopped.

Though I appeared upright and awake, I was actually in a dream state – a walking trance, probably induced by clinical shock. I could only stand there hypnotized - horrified, by what I was looking at. This could not possibly be real! I *had* to be dreaming. And, if it was a dream, then there had to be some way to wake up! Some noise or something from the "other" world I really belonged in, that would bring me awake.

Should it turn out I was *not* dreaming, I was going to need some real answers in a hurry – because that meant that Life, specifically *my* life, was completely insane. I simply could not grasp how or why this could even be happening - and this poor young priest was the person who was supposed to explain it all. And that's why, when he looked back at me and solemnly said "It is not always ours to know the reason why", I could only stare at him in disbelief, as if <u>he</u> were the crazy one! I half expected him to finish with, *"...and into the valley of death rode the noble six-hundred"*.

My already paralyzing confusion became irritation, then anger, as I kept digesting the words he had spoken. He had been reduced to just another variation of that over-used religious platitude: *"The Lord works in strange and mysterious ways"* - as if everyone in that room could not already see that!

But, even worse, essentially he was telling me that he – the only person there who was an acknowledged source of spiritual understanding - was as clueless as I was! At least, about the only thing that mattered to any of us in that room. And in that moment, he became just one more well-dressed, well-meaning confused human - in a room that was already chock full of them.

It has been said: If we want to actually *know* God - as opposed to knowing about or simply believing - we must release all of our preconceived notions of what that actually means. We must let go of our comfortable and comforting assumptions, even long-held beliefs.

Sooner or later most of us figure out that many of our genuine board-certified religious teachers, even those with advanced degrees from some highly respected "Divinity School"(?) may not actually *know* what it is they appear to know a great deal about. In other words, deeply held religious beliefs, even when embraced by millions of souls, or handed down for millennia, are just not the same thing as the *experience* they address. Real spiritual knowledge (and there definitely is such a thing!) transcends and completes <u>all</u> religions, without ever demeaning or diminishing any.

But, designer suits and fabulous robes, even when topped off with a really interesting hat (all the aptly named "trappings of the priesthood"), often disguise or obscure an actual absence of substance. And this is what I was in the process of learning – very painfully. And, while everyone there knew Doris was dead far too young, and all of us agreed that this was an unspeakably terrible thing, only I knew what we had actually experienced. And the true implications of that were not going to become clear to anyone, least of all me, for a very long time.

You don't have to go to sleep,
to wake up in a nightmare!

Doris and I had stopped for gas on our way out of town. We were on our way to an Air Force Radar Site less than an hour outside of my hometown, where I had just spent the final two years of my enlistment, when I noticed an old elementary school friend we called "Digger" walking by. We had not seen each other since the 8th grade and I was excited and happy just to see someone from the old neighborhood.

It was said that Joe "Digger" O'Dea and his dad helped dig graves for Marley's Funeral Home - or something like that - hence his nickname. (Kids will gladly fill in any details in your personal identity for you.)

I told "Digger" I was headed for Benton Air Force base to sign out on a 30 day leave that would culminate on the exact day my four-year tour would be up, so we were celebrating my discharge early. I asked if he would like to go along for the ride and he jumped in.

We were all in my little sky-blue and white Hillman 'Husky', a small station-wagon type import that was built on the same chassis as a Nash Metropolitan. The two front bucket seats each sat on four metal legs, hinged at the base of the front legs, so that the whole seat rocked forward when someone needed get into or out of the rear seat. Digger had a bad left leg, a knee that didn't bend completely, so he sat sideways behind Doris, stretching his left leg out across the back seat.

Benton Air Force Station sat on the top of Red Rock Mountain, about thirty miles outside of Wilkes-Barre in Northeastern Pennsylvania. The Radar Site was in the heart of the lush Pocono Mountains, with a large clear mountain lake, Lake Jean, within walking distance – and, it was only about a forty-minute drive from my home.

My well-connected CBS Radio Washington Bureau-Chief and brother, Jim, had arranged a "Humanitarian Reassignment" for me. Less than two years earlier, my Mom had passed-away (at 42!) while taking a nap, leaving my two little sisters, 12 and 3, to care for. I would be close enough to live at home and commute and help provide some emotional support.

When Joe got in the car, I apologized for not having seat belts in the back, as the car hadn't come with any. I had just that day installed one on the driver's side and had one for the passenger's with me in the car.

I lived off-base and drove the 30 miles each way to work every day on the back roads and small highways of northeastern Pennsylvania. I was going to install Doris' in a day or so, before we left town on our postponed honeymoon, even though she laughingly but adamantly insisted she would never wear it.

Working out of the Provost Sergeant's Office, I was well aware of the many car accidents, too many of them fatal, on the winding mountain road I traversed every day. I'd had to process a few of them during my time there. The zig-zag highway up and down the mountain was infamous for collisions with "suicide deer", and other single car accidents. Most of them were due to fog from the clouds at the top of the mountain, plus rain, snow, ice, or alcohol – too often, all of the above.

After the beautiful drive through the Pennsylvania farmland and pristine countryside to the base, the signing of the leave-book, and a quick tour for Joe and Doris of the place I'd spent my last two years, we headed back to town. I was not going to miss going up and down that steep twisting mountain road one bit. The view from the top and the state park at the bottom were incredibly beautiful, with a series of waterfalls and a hiking trail beside them all the way down from Lake Jean to the valley below. Driving the mountain, however, was an entirely different experience.

We stopped at the lovely old hotel-restaurant that sat just down the road from the foot of the mountain. I knew I would probably not see any of this again except for the very last day of our honeymoon when I would sign back in from leave, and out of the Air Force forever. It was late afternoon as we went in and had lunch, washing it down with a celebratory "Bloody Mary" apiece, and some early

60's Rock & Roll from the juke-box. All in all, a perfect way to mark the end of four years of military service while renewing a childhood friendship.

Leaving the restaurant and cruising joyfully down life's highway through some of the most beautiful country in the world, I remember being almost overwhelmed with happiness, naturally and completely in the moment. My four very long years in the Air Force were finally over!

Now, I don't mean to imply I was not grateful for the opportunity to serve our country. It was a very special time, 1960 to 64, but I had come to that quiet little Radar Site from a Fighter/Interceptor Squadron that had solid-fuel nuclear tipped air-to-air missiles "locked and loaded" on the "5 minute birds", and security was as high as it gets – all day, every day.

While *lethal force* was obviously not encouraged, it was definitely acknowledged. As the pilots, R/O's and ground crews all agreed: "Better a small hole in someone stupid, than a large hole in the east coast."

Thus, on my very first day at my new duty station beginning the 4 to 12 shift, I unfortunately "jacked-up" the base's "First Sergeant" because he didn't have his ID pass upon exiting. After Air Police School and 2 years of guarding a squadron of hot-rod F-101 "Voodoo's" charged with protecting the skies over Washington, Philadelphia and New York – and without "personal recognition", since he and I had yet to meet – and with no proper ID to be on the base? Well, it was weapon drawn, and "Up against the wall on your fingertips and toes, sir, until I can verify your identity and clearance". It took a few moments for him to realize I was completely serious, which then led to an explosion of sputtering and invective, screaming threats complete with promises that I "...would not _ever_ receive a promotion, no matter how long you are stationed here – not even if you stay for 20 years!" In his world, I would die an "E-3" – or even lower, if he could drum up something to bust me for! On the base, everybody liked me. I was personable, funny, and good at what I did – once I eventually got the hang of the, everyone-knows-everyone, "family" atmosphere. But not the _First Shirt_.

Let us just say, Sgt. Smith made those last two years seem a whole lot longer, especially with all the real family issues I had to deal with anyway. So, meeting Doris, becoming husband and wife, and being freed from his sphere of influence – well, I was more than a little happy to say good-bye.

It also meant I would never need to strap on the old ".45" and night-stick again. No more midnight-to-eight shifts, drinking 12-hour-old-coffee to stay awake. No more spit-shining anything. And no more "suicide-deer" accident reports to fill out!

Truth be told, my whole past was coalescing into one long slowly fading preamble to an as yet undefined, but very bright, future. I could see nothing on the horizon but some well-deserved happiness for us both - sleeping in with my new bride, blissfully discovering each other. (Did I mention we were both virgins when we met?)

I would just collect some "unemployment" until the Pennsylvania State Police Academy began – and that might take months! We didn't need much money, life was good. We were already living in our own little heaven-on-earth!

We took the back road toward the old Huntsville Dam just to appreciate the many miles of farmland covered in white, and the ice-and-snow-covered reservoir. The road itself was mostly clean and dry, with just a thin layer of well-packed leftover snow in a few places. Some recently plowed snow banks, almost as high as the roof of our little car, were along the sides of the road.

During a Northeastern Pennsylvania winter, it can snow any number of times before it ever gets warm enough for some of it to melt. "No hurry, no worry" was always the way, around those parts, especially during the winter.

Just as we are coming over a rise on the narrow two-lane road, a large black sedan pointed in the same direction as us starts to pull out of the old country gas station ahead on our left. It quickly becomes apparent he's attempting to make a U-Turn in order to head back in the direction we are approaching from – and that he doesn't see us! He was facing the opposite way, and hasn't yet looked our way, even though he is about to cross into our lane.

In an instant, I become hyper-alert. Time slows down as I begin to downshift in order to keep traction while I'm braking. We were only doing about 35 mph, and we're slowing. He is throwing snow up off his back wheels, spinning his tires and just having fun in an old 'tank' of a 1940's sedan on this little used back road.

I try to get onto the shoulder of the road on my right, but there is a wall of snow, and already he is filling the center of the narrow two-lane road, leaving room for only half of our little car on either side. By the time he sees us and tries to move to his right, there is nowhere left for us to go. We collide almost head on, our left front fenders hitting each other almost perfectly.

I remember being thankful Doris and Joe were both on the side away from the impact, as our fenders absorbed most of the shock and my seat belt prevented me from being thrown into the steering wheel. It is not a particularly violent collision. I'd seen many far worse. I look over at Doris and she is still sitting in her seat, but her chin is resting on her chest and she appears to be unconscious. Strange, we could not have been doing more than 15 or 20 when we hit. Joe is asking if we are OK. I put my hands under her chin, calling softly to her, "Honey?" I lift her head up toward me to pat her cheeks and attempt to wake her up, and when I lift it, it comes right up off her shoulders.

It's no longer connected to her body, and only the vertebrate keep it from coming off completely in my hands.

I cannot comprehend the image I'm seeing. I feel as if I am dreaming. Time stops. Everything is silent, perfectly still. I can't move.

I look at her face. Her eyes are closed as if she's sleeping. Not a mark anywhere, except her head and her body are no longer connected. I watch blood trickle from her severed jugular vein, my mind is paralyzed with horror. I simply cannot accept what I am seeing.

Out of the corner of my eye, I see the windshield. There is a large hole in it, directly in front of her. My God! Sitting sideways behind her, maybe reflexively putting his hands on the back of her seat, Joe must have been thrown forward even at 15 or 20 mph, plus whatever the other car's speed was at the moment of impact, and his weight and inertia had pushed her seat, and her, into the windshield . . . and down.

This can't be! My God! I've *got* to be dreaming! I pull her body towards me and hold her close, tightly. Resting her head on my chest and shoulder, like we fall asleep every night, telling her softly and emphatically that I love her, that everything will be all right - as if saying it will somehow make it happen, make what I just saw go away - but even my voice sounds very far away. From that moment on, "I" am gone from this world.

I am in some bizarre nightmare version of my life, and yet I appear to be awake - it will be a very long time before that changes.

I sit back and lay her down gently on my lap, stroking her hair and talking to her. Still not able to accept, to process, what I am seeing. Slowly, I unbuckle my seat-belt and slide gently out of the car, softly laying her down on my seat. I tell her that I have to leave for a moment, to go inside the gas station and call an ambulance. I can't bring myself to close the door as I walk away.

The driver of the other car is coming toward me as I walk zombie-like toward the gas station office. He is just a kid, maybe 17, saying something about how "...my girlfriend banged her leg on the dash-board, but she's not really hurt. Are you ok?" His words make no sense to me, and for some reason I just say, softly, "If my wife dies, I'm going to kill you, right here." I don't really mean it. And she is very obviously (to anyone but me) already dead. But I just can't accept that, and don't know what else to say.

I feel like I am in some nightmare-theater, watching from far away a gruesome play being acted out. As if from a distance I hear myself tell the man in the gas station office to "Call an ambulance, please. And hurry." I turn away from his questioning eyes and head back to the car. He appears to think it was a "fender-bender" and is surprised someone needs an ambulance.

She's lying just as I left her, the door still slightly ajar. I open it the rest of the way and kneel down on the hard snow, kissing her hair and talking to her. Still unable to process the full meaning of what is before me. For the first of what will be many times, I pinch my arm. Hard. I can't feel any pain.

Nothing changes. I dig my nails into the soft skin on the bottom of my wrist and forearm, hard enough to break the skin and draw blood. I can't seem to wake up! Finally, I see myself do the most extraordinary thing. I reach across Doris to the glove compartment and take out my duty notepad and pen, and get up and proceed to "work" the accident!

Drawing a precise diagram of what occurred, I note the time of day, describe the color of the sky; the weather; the lighting; tire and skid marks; estimated speed of both vehicles.

For those minutes until the ambulance arrives, I am not the person *in* the accident. I'm just "working" it. Trying to do something, anything, to bring some sense into a situation that (*Dear God, please!*) cannot possibly be real! Attempting desperately to function "calmly and professionally in any emergency", as I had been taught and trained, I hear the voice of one of my old Air Police School instructors: "People will be looking to the officer at the scene for direction." Really?

Well, not today, pal! I am absolutely the last guy on earth that anyone should be getting any directions from. I just want to wake up - right now! *Anywhere else!*

By now, Digger has gotten out of the car -- and I never see him again, to this day! Perhaps he was at the wake or funeral. If he did come, most of the time I would not have been able to tell. I remember looking for him so I could assure him it was not his fault. To this day, even as I write this, I can only hope he knows.

I remember the medics from the Ambulance asking me where I was hurt. There was blood all over the front of me, but I didn't have a scratch. The steering wheel - and my seat belt! - had kept me from any harm. I will live with that forever.

Of the first days immediately after the accident, the funeral preparations, eating, where (or even if) I slept, I have absolutely no memory. All of it is lost in the fog of shock. There is at least a week that is a complete blank.

I don't even remember the funeral and burial. I have a vague memory of 'watching' - observing without being a part - as the people and places came and went, as if in some far-away movie.

My only true memory of the time immediately following the accident is noteworthy simply because it was the first emotion strong enough to pierce the mind-numbing state I had been walking around in.

Standing at the coffin with our priest, the very same guy who had just married us, hearing myself angrily stage-whispering much too loudly to this poor equally confused man:

"What!"

"What the hell does *that* mean?"

(Pause)

"Are you telling me you don't know any more about this than I do?"

(He looks down at the floor, avoiding my eyes.)

"Then why are you dressed like that?"

"Why are we even standing here?"

I was completely serious. It made absolutely no sense to me.

After a lifetime in the Catholic faith, I had already heard every variation on *"The Lord works in strange and mysterious ways"*. Our religion was a tangible part of our life, and not just the many rituals.

It seemed, at least as a child, as if every other day was some kind of "Holy Day", the feast of some saint, or the celebration of some other long ago historic religious occurrence. My brother, Tom, was an altar boy throughout most of our childhood together. He even went on to the Maryknoll Seminary to study for the priesthood. We had a cousin who was already a priest (now a *Monsignor*) and an aunt who started out to be a nun, but chose to be a nurse.

Only two years before, when my mother took a nap with my three-year-old sister and never woke up again (at 42!), "strange and mysterious ways" is what they told us. And that's pretty much what was said about *anything* too difficult to understand - simply accept it as "God's inscrutable will".

Well, that was not going to be good enough this time. Not even close!

When the truly incomprehensible dissolves your reality in an instant, you immediately develop an insatiable appetite for REALITY! No matter what it might look like - or what it might cost. You need *something* that makes sense of the absurd – anything! – and you need it now!

The first thing any of us wants to know in those moments is, "Why?" Why is this happening? Why do things like this happen, period? Rational people want a reason for their pain. First, so they can cease doing whatever it is that is causing it, if that's at all possible. That part is just human nature.

But there is something else. Just behind the rational mind, our deeper selves know there is a harmony to life! The Soul *knows* it is part of a greater whole, *knows* that there really is "Something". Something, not just imagined or believed in.

It's what inspires us, even on the human or personality level, to connect with others outside of ourselves. Looking outward for what we feel unconsciously deep within us. Whether it's joining a "club" or a gang when we are children; later, a sports team we might choose to cheer for; our country, or even our religion as we mature. Whatever, the "self" longs to be a part of something greater than the ego.

And the bigger the better! It's also why "family" is so important in virtually all civilized cultures.

Nature itself is infinitely more complex than any of our singular lives. Yet Nature is, from the microscopic to the galactic, absolute harmonious balance, perfection in action, everything working together! And we, as individuals and collectively, are obviously and inextricably a part of that.

Nobody knows - especially, why?

So, if such an event as I was experiencing is to be accepted as "a part of God's plan", we are left with two very provocative questions: First: What the hell kind of God would want to emotionally devastate and frighten the living bejeezus out of His own offspring? [*Great word, "bejeezus", more on that later.*]

And second: If this actually *is* part of some Divine Plan, then what are we supposed to learn from such an experience? What is the purpose? Exactly what is it we are supposed to acquire from such enormous pain, and how will it, or even should it, shape our future?

Which also brings to mind the question:

What future!?

That place within where our future had been envisioned, where our dreams were nurtured? A little home, perhaps some children, all those bright sunny days ahead filled with happiness and discovery – none of that existed anymore, not even as a dream!

My life had *become* a dream, a really bad dream. By any stretch of the imagination, it was an absolute nightmare of the worst kind - the kind that begins all over again every time you wake up. To reference an otherwise wonderful movie, I appeared to be starring in, *"Groundhog Day - in Hell!"*

There would be no more moments of Doris and Michael in their little home, deep in innocent love. That whole 'reality' was in as many pieces as the windshield - gone forever in a nightmare of blood and broken glass.

Tomorrow? Tomorrow was a void. A dark emptiness, filled with foreboding. Jesus! *Anything* could happen! At any moment!

That was the only thing I really <u>knew</u> – and I knew it beyond a shadow of a doubt.

What I did *not* know was that I had just been catapulted into what St. John of The Cross referred to as, *The Dark Night of the Soul.* Something I had never even heard of, although it was the title of a well-known book that the good Father had no doubt read in seminary. Unfortunately, it was a concept I would not even be exposed to for years to come.

But, ignorance offered me no immunity. There I was anyway. Standing on the very path the book describes, completely oblivious to the nature of the journey before me. It was a journey that would eventually teach me things about we humans that neither the good Father nor I could have even imagined – although they were probably the very things he had become a priest to learn!

Still, I would wager that very few of his seminary teachers really understood the price we are asked to pay in order to apprehend such "knowledge", although I have no doubt they believed they did. After all, it takes some very serious inspiration, coupled with intense desire and no small amount of courage, to aspire to the title of "Spokesperson for God."

One does not get to be a Catholic priest without first having "the calling", which then requires eschewing one's former life and friends and embracing the pattern: Vows of *Poverty* (albeit, in the wealthiest religion on earth); *Abstinence* (along with some legendary lapses of virtue); and *Obedience* (which too often means to the Pope or the Bishop rather than the Inner Divine). Unquestionably, the Catholic clergy was *not* an easy path.

Still, while our priests and nuns had established a healthy "working" relationship, most did not really *know* God. Witness even the posthumous confessions of the saintly Mother Theresa. For those whose vows included obedience to Rome in times of spiritual confusion, the Bishop was just a phone call away. Hell, compared to God way up in heaven somewhere, the Pope is right around the corner! Close enough.

Well, not for some of us.

There is a man, one Paul Levy, who experienced the very same mental and emotional trauma I would eventually go through, and he has written lucidly of his experience – unfortunately, I did not hear of him in time to save myself an enormous amount of suffering, but I will share his wisdom with you. What I was about to experience is called the "Shamanic Journey". Brother Paul describes the process this way:

There is an intimate correlation between being traumatized...and having a shamanic initiation /spiritual awakening. Trauma is an experience that is overwhelming to the ego, in that it can't be assimilated by the ego in the typical way. The trauma initiates and catalyzes the deeper process of the archetype of the shaman to begin to formulate and crystallize itself in the unconscious of the future shaman. This precipitates a deeper part of the psyche to become mobilized, as the shamans journey deep inside themselves, flying on the wings of their creative imagination to address and become acquainted with what has gotten activated within them.

The shaman's descent into the darkness can be agonizing, a veritable crucifixion. To quote Jung: "The shaman's experience of...death and regeneration implies, at a higher level, the idea of being made whole through sacrifice...in a word, apotheosis - elevated from an ordinary person to a 'god'."

In the 1964 world I found myself in, there were no Shamans to guide or enlighten. Had there been, that poor priest and I would have warmly welcomed any of them joining us in our *dance macabre!* As it was, the words of Jesus - "If a man would have life, he must die" or, "If a man would save his life, he must first lose it"; culminating in, "Know ye not that ye are Gods?" – would have made all the sense in the world! Not particularly comfortable, but comforting.

As usual, old Jesus was just trying not to sugar-coat the uncomfortable fact He had come to demonstrate. We really must "die" in order to reintegrate our mind and soul, remember our own inescapable oneness with God. As Jesus himself was fond of pointing out, there are any number of ways to "die", and the really good ones don't require the actual death of the body – only our attachment to it, and identification with it.

[You will want to stop and meditate on that last sentence.]

Unfortunately, that crucial perspective was far off in my future. At that precise moment, the only "me" I had ever known was already quite dead. "Air Policeman" Michael, "State Trooper-to-be" Michael, "blissful husband of the beautiful Doris" Michael, all were just as dead as Doris herself.

In retrospect, it would have been nice if my ego-dissolution could have been, say, just a little more gradual, (the actual plan for all our lives.) Losing in an instant everything I knew myself to be, or hoped to ever become, was truly traumatizing. Like most of us here on Earth, I only knew myself as who I had been, or what I was hoping to become. And they were both, for all intents and purposes, in the coffin with Doris.

As the reality of my situation began to dawn on me, I looked around the large funeral parlor and understood for the first time that I was the only person like me in that room.

Oh, everyone else looked just as sad and confused as I was. But, I am absolutely certain I was the only one just barely keeping at bay the overwhelming urge to scream as loud as I could:

"What the hell is going on here!?"

And then, running as fast as possible, burst out through the Funeral Home doors – hoping that I might somehow burst back into my "real" life. I swear - every evening until her burial - it was all I could do not to do that.

Looking around each night, the funeral home always seemed to be filled mostly with friends from either my childhood or the Air Force. Many of us, just a couple years ago, were 1950's teenagers together. Those of us from my childhood had grown up in Norman Rockwell's beautifully illustrated world of walking to school together, with daily after school sandlot baseball or football (played on a real sand-lot with plenty of actual dirt and red sand). Then, a short hike up into the Pocono Mountains, walking through an Eden-like existence to crystal-clear streams, where running water carved swimming holes out of ancient rock. Places called "The Tubs", or "Flat Rock"(*aka* "bare-ass-beach").

Wasn't that just yesterday? What the hell are we doing in a funeral home? This stuff was for our grandparents, or aunts and uncles, people who had already had rich full lives.

My voice began to rise from the sheer frustration of asking "The Big Questions of Life" of someone who, I had just discovered, was <u>not</u> going to answer them. So, along with the anger and frustration, anxiety was beginning to well up in me. It began to occur to me that I did not know *anyone* else to ask these questions of. Who else could possibly have the knowledge he had been studying all his adult life?

"So, that's it, Father? *'The Lord works in strange ways'*? For Christ's sake, do you think I can't *see* that! We can <u>all</u> see that – *Jesus, man! That's my wife laying there!*"

Oh, dear. Taking the Lord's name in vain - angry, loud, and in public - to a priest! Well, if God doesn't follow any rules, then how the hell are we supposed to?

I could not have known it at the time, but this was actually my first exposure to being "purified in the fire". It was the initial step in the cleansing of my still young mind of the well intentioned (but often erroneous) ideas long ago imposed on my open and trusting child self. Ideas and accepted beliefs about just what it is that God truly requires of us, and desires for us, all of us. Also, who does (and who does not) know the real answers to "Life's persistent questions."   [Thank you Garrison K.]

The truth will <u>definitely</u> set you free . . . . . eventually.

Regardless of the decades-long, and undoubtedly sincere, attempts of assorted nuns and priests to introduce us, I had never actually *met*

Jesus. Or Mother Mary, or "God, the Father", or for that matter, Yahweh, Buddha, Allah, Ram, etc. - nor had I ever met *anyone*, as near as I could tell, who actually had.

We all blissfully assume that the people we entrust with our eternal Souls . . . *actually know what the hell they are talking about!*

Which brings us to the biggest and most bizarre fallacy perpetrated on us by our religious institutions: That the One God there can only possibly be is somehow "different" for each religion! And, that one GOD is apparently in an eternal battle with the other versions of His or Her own infinite Self for some kind of Divine Supremacy, all in order to save *your* Soul and to protect and glorify *your* religion! And, *your* God - whichever name you identify with - is the only "real" one, and vastly superior (no doubt in mysterious ways) to all those other versions!

Well, as they say today – WTF?!

How can anyone possibly believe that? Well, just look around you . . . and this is the 21st Century!

As I turned and left the Funeral Home, filled with our families and friends, I could feel their eyes following me, hear the whispers: "Poor guy, it was just a matter of time."; "Well, that's been coming for awhile."

My paralyzing confusion seems to have been mistaken for some sort of brave stoicism. Apparently no one had any idea just how crazy I really was.

But I was also frightened, and very much alone, and I would soon begin latching onto whatever floated by on my "Great Dark Ocean of Unknowing", grasping at anything that might keep me from drowning in it. Just surrendering and letting go meant real insanity, and I was still reeling from my first taste of that. The memory of the aftermath of the collision, the pictures still burning in my mind were truly insane. You can imagine anything, momentarily, and then it will go away. But an actual experience is indelible, and never really leaves. By any measure this was an absolute horror, and it happened in my very real (at least until then) life.

Walking around in the exact same world we had just inhabited together in our warm and gentle love was, at best, surreal. At its worst it was a walking nightmare, and there seemed to be no way to wake up from it.

I had been given some sleeping pills by one of the medics from the base, but for some reason, I couldn't take them. Alcohol was "normal" for my family and friends, so an aspirin or an Alka-Seltzer to fend off a hangover was also considered normal. But *pills* were just not done. Not by anyone I knew. A prescription was usually the sign of a serious problem. [My, how far we've come.] Still, I saved the sleeping pills - just in case.

With Irish and German parents, there was almost always real Irish whiskey and genuine German beer somewhere nearby. That is what we knew. Now, alone and over 21, I began to drink myself to sleep virtually every night - mental and physical exhaustion were not enough to stop the thoughts and questions in my mind. Alcohol numbed the pain and kept the visions at a distance. And, since waking up was when the nightmares actually *began*, I quickly became an utter disaster happening in slow motion.

Had I begun taking those sleeping pills then, with "The 60's" just beginning to flower, I'd have easily, probably enthusiastically, become a "junkie" - and most assuredly dead in a very short time. Sleep (actually unconsciousness, anyway it could be achieved) was a blessing. A few hours of relief from the constant pain of being trapped in a life that was just this side of a trip to the funhouse. When I would wake up, I would pray before I even opened my eyes that what I thought I was remembering was really just an exceptionally bad dream.

This time when I reach over, she will be there.

Then it would all begin again, hugging her pillow and burying my face in it, breathing deeply of the pillowcase I could not bring myself to wash. Smelling her, imagining it was her, and sobbing deep convulsive sobs that would curl my body as if I was collapsing into myself, screaming into her pillow so as not to frighten the neighbors, sounding like some horribly wounded animal. Holding the pillow tightly, as if it were her body, begging whatever lunatic God there was to please, *please* bring her back . . . . . . or take <u>me</u>! Yes, that would be good! *Please,* just take me out of here. Let me be with her, please!

Oh, God - how I wanted to die!

Sometimes I would go to our old church, Holy Savior, back in "East End", where I grew up. I would go to confession and then an early morning mass with the fewest people. There I would receive communion, and take the pills – all of them!

After everyone else had left the church I would tearfully begin to apologize to God for destroying my own life, for not being able to take the pain of the visions in my mind. Then, with the pills in my hand ready to swallow, I would remember, actually see, Father James McCauliffe addressing my graduating 8th Grade class about the evils of the world we were about to enter as 1950's teenagers. Looking all around the class, from person to person, he would declare in his thick Irish brogue about the shame of girls wearing make-up ("You'll not be receivin' the Holy Host from me on Sunday, with lipstick on your lips!"), or skirts above the bottom of the knee, smoking, alcohol, immoral behavior of all kinds. And then, looking directly at me in the middle of the classroom, his face florid from having worked himself into a frenzy of righteous judgment and condemnation, Irish brogue in full-flower: "And if you take your own life, you will go *dir-r-rectly* to Hell! And you'll burn there, *forever!*" He scared me so badly I told my mother when I got home from school! I had no idea why he did that. Of course, I do now - it would save my life a decade later. Guaranteed!

My fear of Hell and damnation - the gift of Father McCauliffe and my strict Catholic upbringing - saved my life. One thing I *was* certain of, beyond a shadow of a doubt, was that she was <u>not</u> in Hell.

Therefore, if I killed myself - no matter how good it might feel to end that pain - I would go "*dir-r-r-rectly to Hell, forever!*" I didn't believe Hell could cause me any more pain than I woke up with every day – but it meant that I would never, *ever* see her again! Hell was forever I was taught - and I believed! And after agonizing for a time, I would tearfully put the pills back in my pocket, slowly dragging myself out of the church like some forlorn zombie. Up to my eyeballs in Hell, already - and no way out.

What had we done to deserve this? What had I done, even unknowingly? What could *she* possibly have done - that gentle, always smiling, fairy-like creature of constant kindness - angels must pray to one day be like her. She should have lived forever! Where do things like this come from? And, for the ten-thousandth time, *why*?

There would be small breakthroughs. One was a particularly vivid catharsis that helped completely change the way I approached life itself.

It was late, and I was standing in our living room holding what was left of a bottle of cheap whiskey by the neck in my left hand. My other hand was clenched in a fist, wanting to lash out, to strike back at something, while Ray Charles sang "I Can't Stop Loving You" in the background, for the hundredth time. I was crying, sobbing - and screaming at God to, please, either "Help me - or take me too! *Now!*"

"In the name of Jesus, *do not leave me here like this!*"

Silence.

"God damn it! You appeared to Moses, and the apostles, the children at Fatima! *I know you can do it!*" Crying, "I just want to talk to you."

"Please, just help me understand."

Sobbing..."God, Father, Mother Mary, *please.* I can't take it anymore."

Silence . . .

Slowly, in that last long awful silence, my feelings toward "The Almighty" began to change. The pain, the dark emptiness was being filled with a horrible drunken rage, a seething hateful anger - at God Himself!

He could do it if He wanted to! It is what I had been taught all my life. He had done it for the apostles . . . and others . . . saints and sinners alike! Saul of Tarsus/Paul the Apostle! Persecutor of Christians, for Christ's sake.

So, He had to be choosing not to!

The logic was impeccable!

Swaying drunkenly in the middle of our living room floor, with hot tears burning my face, through clenched teeth I swore slowly at Him: "All right . . . All right, you crazy son-of-a-bitch! You have either caused this to happen, or You have allowed it to happen." My voice rose, "*And neither* of these is acceptable! *Not for her!*" Louder: "*She did not deserve to die! Especially like that!*" Screaming, "*Answer me, goddamn You!*

The echo of my words rang in the room, and in my head. My blood was pounding, loud.

Then, slowly, in a hoarse whisper, as cold as ice: "All right. All right . . . you lunatic bastard. One day, sooner or later, *I* am going to die! And then *I* am going to be in *your* world! And, you will *have* to deal with me!"

Yelling, "I will hunt you down! I <u>will</u> find You!!!"

Screaming, "*Do You hear me?!*"

It was like vomiting up all the repressed anger, the mental and emotional frustration, the pain and the insanity of it all. Hating, and screaming at the "Loving Father, God" I had been begging and pleading to, virtually every waking moment for these many days and weeks --- and most of my life.

My head began to spin. I felt empty. The only thing that had been able to penetrate the darkness I lived in and engage my shattered mind had been taken to its earthly end. I tried imagining what I would do to God, if and when I finally found Him.

But there was only Ray, still moaning in pain in the background, in perfect harmony with my own suffering, and the floor rising up to meet me - where I would awake the next morning.

I assume I was taken out of my body before I said or did something truly irreparable - even for God. I was capable of that. I was capable of anything...

And that was the great lesson to be learned! (God help us all if it can only be learned that way): We _are_ capable of <u>absolutely anything</u> when we are in that kind of pain. Especially if we no longer have any idea of what actual 'right' and 'wrong' might be!

Call it a kind of superimposed "supernatural existentialism", if you will.

The <u>gift</u> of such trauma, and it is a priceless treasure, is that we are still left with the overwhelming desire to reunite with the Love that was lost – and, most importantly, *the ability to endure absolutely anything to get there!*

The loss of the love of your life - or your child, a beloved parent, even a truly good friend, especially when unexpected - can turn you into a serious "spiritual seeker". Even if you didn't know there was such a thing. Unfortunately, most people do *not* know that true spiritual awareness, the knowledge or Gnosis of their own soul, is something that can and should be sought - let alone that it might actually be found, and experienced!

So, when a very important part of you is suddenly no longer in this world, yet they're still very much alive *in* you . . . well, *where exactly is that?*

Charlie and the brotherhood of "lost" souls

I chose to stay in our little apartment alone with my pain. My father wanted me to move back home, come back to the old neighborhood for support, but I was in no condition to try to explain to either my younger sisters or anyone else what I was going through. It was apparent that neither I nor anyone I knew would be able to find words that helped, or even made sense. I just felt deeply that I needed to be alone.

I needed to be where we had lived and loved, surrounded by the things we had shared. True, it was merely the setting of a reality that was no more, but it was all I had. It was the only reality I had left. That little 'three-rooms-and-a-bath' walk-up on the other side of my hometown was more than just a cheap apartment. It was the landscape of our shared life, witness to our love. Everything in it was *ours*. Nothing but our clothes had come from our past lives. We created it together, and only got to live in it for those few months.

I was nowhere near the "letting go" stage of grief. I felt I absolutely *had* to be surrounded by the things that were "ours". Unfortunately, that was a two-edged sword. A constant reminder that, while she was there in everything I saw, and I could *feel* closer to her there than anywhere else, I still could not tangibly see her or touch her.

A big part of me, as with most of us at that time in our lives, only knew the physical-world part of ourselves. Like most of us, we never really thought about or analyzed the nature of our love - the power of a shared thought or feeling; the joy that would rise up within when we would come together after any time apart; the knowing the needs of the other without words. It seems the well-meaning folks who saw to our early religious upbringing forgot to mention the most important part: "The Lord thy God is One." Love = Oneness! We were part of each other!

I would attempt to learn to use the warmth in my heart that thinking of our time together brought me, to assuage the ever-present heartache. When I would think of our moments together, it was like dreaming while awake. I would be filled with her warmth and love, sometimes inadvertently laughing aloud from the sheer joy that came from the memory of us together. But then, the sound of my laughter would bring me back to the present, and I would remember how I saw her in the car, her head in my hands, eyes closed.

And in that moment the world would again become dark and insane, a crazy place that set my mind on fire, and made my chest hurt as if a hot knife had been stuck in it. In those moments it was hard to even breathe. I recall many times actually struggling to draw a deep breath, as if I could not get enough air into my lungs.

Then, our apartment was not a place I should be in. Everything was her, and she was nowhere to be found - an endless cycle of exhaustion, sleep, and awakening again to pain and confusion.

Across the street from our apartment was an old neighborhood tavern I had not previously ventured into. We were still "newlyweds", so any night out usually meant just the two of us walking down the block for a pizza or something. We were a long way from needing time away from each other or to be with others - but, now? I began to realize I could not be alone always. I was aware I needed the company of others, but only those who didn't really know me. Those who knew me chose to avoid me because they did not know what to say or how to help. I was a constant reminder that Life was not at all as predictable as evryone agreed it was, or it had once appeared to be. So I needed a relatively quiet place, a place where I could be invisible.

"*Charlie Wroblewski's*" appeared, at least from the outside, to be a good place to escape the nasty edge of that sword for a while. Charlie himself, the proprietor, was just one of the Ashley/Newtown Wroblewski's. The rest of the family was busy around the corner with the family business – a Funeral Home! So I could reasonably assume that he would have had at least a passing acquaintance with people like me. He might even be the first person I had met recently that even knew *how* to "be with" a person already in some kind of personal hell. Did he ever!

"Charlie's" was not a busy place. There were a few of the old coal miners that made up a lot of the Anthracite region of that time, drinking away their "black-lung" pensions amidst their assorted friends and neighbors. Some of the regulars still had jobs, some were "looking", some were "collecting", and some would just do whatever needed doing, for a quick buck to get through the day.

Their future, much as I saw my own, was as bleak as the landscape still visible on the edge of town: Huge now defunct "Collieries" where the Anthracite coal the region had once thrived on was cleaned and separated into the different sizes, all of it fed by miles of now rusted and overgrown railroad tracks and worn out two-lane tar & macadam roads.

Most of the surrounding mountains and hilltops looked as if they had been imported from the moon, strip-mined and bereft of any life save for a tiny handful of grass or a half dead shrub. Here and there, a scraggly death-defying White Birch sapling would stand alone in the middle of acres of black shale and rock, incongruously sticking out of a hillside at a crazy angle.

Death was an acknowledged part of life here. The coal industry had died a few decades ago, so this little town on the edge of Wilkes-Barre was dying. Most of the residents had family and friends who had died in the mines or one of the last three wars, or were themselves dying from mine injuries or black-lung disease.

Even old gravel-voiced Charlie was dying of throat cancer!

I felt right at home.

Charlie was a great bear of a man, with a big shock of unruly white hair and laughing eyes expressing an even bigger personality. He had what a more cosmopolitan soul might describe as great *Jois de vivre,* the Joy of Life! While he was not at all pleased about the cancer diagnosis, especially the ravages of it on his voice, he was still going to laugh, and even sing if he felt like it. He had obviously decided to live each moment left to him with gusto and great joy in the present. He was the sole proprietor and bartender, from open to close. I never saw another person behind the bar. This was where he would make his last stand, and no doubt exit laughing - and singing!

It was a genuine "old time" place even by 1964, weathered graying wood outside with well-worn wooden floors and a long L-shaped bar to the right of the front door. Probably built in the 1930's or earlier, it had carved wooden booths and a juke box in the fairly large back room, and a couple of dart boards and a pool table up front in the bar area. Some former "hot tomato" from twenty or thirty years ago might wander in and order a 7&7 or a *"Cuba Libre"*, but it was pretty much a shot-and-a-beer place for men already older than their years, and their offspring.

For food, what was euphemistically referred to as "Breakfast" was served from opening to closing. It consisted of home-pickled hard-boiled eggs kept in a large jar on the bar, alongside another big jar full of spicy red sausages, also in some kind of pickling juice. The words, "Ham & eggs with home fries!" would get you two sausages, two pickled eggs, and a bag of chips - for a buck! Wash it all down with a 10 cent draft or three, and you were well prepared for a long day of meditating on the slings and arrows of outrageous fortune.

Or, as Charlie would growl, in his Polish flavored "Satchmo" Armstrong voice, *"Why do you think they call it 'harsh reality', pal?"*

In time, Charlie would figure out that I'm the guy in the newspaper a few weeks back and decide to take me under his wing. I was a loner. At a mere 21 years of age, much younger than anyone else there, and I knew not a soul in the place. But, everyone usually sat around in silence anyway, so I fit right in.

In the beginning, Charlie hadn't said much to me. But somewhere along the line of days he apparently decided to share with me what he called "the rules & tools of life", at least as he had found them to be. And he would teach them to me on a 7-foot pool table, thank you very much.

The wisdom he was imparting was almost hidden by his easy manner, and the apparently mundane application of barroom Pool. But it was that application itself - for stakes that ranged from a 10 cent draft to "braggin' rights in this corner of the galaxy" (when he knewI was short of funds) - that allowed for my easy acquiescence to Charlie's tutelage. It also made for a safe and quiet time that included another person, and that was good. I was not alone, and the game allowed us to learn a lot about each other by way of our common objective (though it would not be a "competition" for a long time). I would get to actually know someone who was not from the Air Force or my childhood while developing a new "skill".

This new skill, without my being aware, was going to bestow upon me (at least the way Charlie played!) the opportunity to truly focus on something other than my pain. Something that was meditative, and demanded focused mind-body coordination, great patience, and one hell of an imagination – because in Charlie's own words: "Defense is for football! There's *always* a shot! If you've got the vision, the skill - and the balls! Arrr-harr-harr-harr!"

There was also a little matter of what I shall have to call "intuitive geometry and multi-dimensional physics:" i.e., developing the ability to actually intuit the precise point, angle and force of the cue-tip striking the cue-ball, in order to create the perfect spin (in angle, direction, and velocity) that would cause said cue-ball to strike the object ball in such an exact manner that it would drop into the desired pocket, while at the same time causing the cue-ball to traverse the table and stop in the most suitable position to attempt the next shot.

As testimony to Charlie's teaching (and playing) skills, we would actually play not just "call your shot", the accepted rules in all tournament play, which means describing exactly what you are attempting to do: "5-ball, one bank, in the corner, kiss off your 9". Charlie insisted we also play "Call your next shot"! Meaning not just describing and making the initial shot – but calling which ball you would shoot after that, and into which pocket it would go, and precisely how *that* would also occur!

Now, the logical mind can accept, even understand, all this just by observation. But it cannot tell you, merely by observation, precisely how many foot-pounds of force will be necessary; nor the precise angle, in degrees, of "English" the cue-ball might need; neither can it factor for, in a formula suitable for the situation, the coefficient of resistance that the "banks" [the sides of the playing table], will have on the ball, including the felt of the table's surface. In other words, one has to learn to see and feel in ways we probably never imagined before.

And then, of course, you must act - precisely. Your body moving in *perfect* harmony with your vision, causing what was created in your imagination to actually occur in physical reality. (Sound familiar?)

In order to accomplish all this, you first must relax completely and enter "the quiet". (Charlie's first commandment: "No thinking while shooting!"); "See" your shot, and the next *two* after it; Then, once you visualize what you are trying to do, you need to accept that it will happen, and act without doubt. Everywhere in Life, doubt and fear are our actual opponents. Nobody ever really beats us. We are always playing against ourselves. If we are in harmony with our purpose (whatever it is we have chosen to attempt) and take full advantage of opportunities presented (make the shot and leave ourselves in good position for the next) our "opponent" won't get to "beat" us! But, we must do what *we* can, to the best of our abilities at the time. Growth is constant, if you analyze what you did or didn't do that caused you to miss, or leave yourself poorly. Learn from each failed attempt, and correct yourself. Win or lose, you will be better at what you are attempting because of the experience.

As in most things, competence only comes with practice, experience - which Charlie generously gave me with great pleasure. It consisted of my getting beaten by a real artist, early and often.

He was not a "hustler". Charlie would tell anyone who asked that he was very good - and that you would need to be at the top of *your* game just to stay *in* the game. His technique appeared effortless because he always seemed to have an easy shot. And that was simply because he could stop the cue ball almost exactly where it belonged for the next step in my dismantling. *"If you stay focused, you'll never have a hard shot"*, he would remind me daily.

Of course, since he was the sole proprietor of the establishment, he had probably played thousands of games on that table. No doubt with the same balls, cue, atmosphere, etc., so that everything there was of-a-piece, a oneness. And a very familiar part of his-own-Self! The cue was not just an extension of his hands, but of his mind. Except for the initial break, he *knew* <u>exactly</u> what was going to happen to each ball when he took his shot; where each would end up, probably within a few inches; where the cue ball would stop, probably less than that, and so on.

He did all this without ego or malice, he merely loved doing this deceptively 'simple' thing as well as he could do it - perhaps as well as it could be done. I sincerely believe that had the world champion of 8-Ball (and I've often watched them on ESPN) wandered into his joint, and Charlie wasn't busy behind the bar, the World Champ would have his hands full - and a far less than even chance of winning. Truth.

But, at least in the beginning, I was as terrible as he was beautiful. So I can honestly say it was a "terrible beauty" with which I learned that, especially in the game of life, you haven't lost until you quit trying. And experience is *the* only real teacher. Which is exactly why we came here, and why the words "terrible beauty" would make perfect sense of most of my life...someday.

Slowly, I came to know some of the regulars, and eventually got good enough to hold my own against most. But, it would be a very long time, even playing him every day, before I would ever win a game against Charlie. He pulled no punches and gave nothing away.

My frustration, and wonder, would grow by the game. The repeated defeats - beheld in quiet awe and amazement – were merely how I learned. It was humbling (bordering on humiliating) but Charlie never let me feel that. A kind word, with some fatherly encouragement, were all he ever spoke – except when I simply forgot to cut my hair. Frankly, I just didn't care enough to think about it. Plus, the Beatles had recently come to America, and it didn't seem to be a problem for them. However, this place was decidedly *not* Liverpool or Greenwich Village, and I did catch a lot of good-natured hell. Difficult as it may be to believe, I did not even notice it was longer than it "should be", I really just didn't care – about very much of anything.

As it grew, though, and when Charlie needed to admonish me for doing something I should have known better than, he would growl very pointedly; "You oughta know better than that by now, Mary!" And then laugh that gargling death-rattle laugh of his. Behind his bluster, he was very kind, and very, very good, so that, conversely, an appreciative - "Great shot, Mary!" - was like a trophy.

After a while, we all got used to the hair – later I even added a goatee. Charlie then decided I must be the first "Bippy" - a combination 50's Beatnik and 60's Hippy.

On a good day, when we were the only ones in the bar, he would usually tell me what he was attempting to do, and, more importantly, precisely how. He was kind enough to suggest to me what I might be doing "wrong", but without ever making me feel as if I had actually done anything wrong. His advice was always a teacher's love for the beauty of the thing he knows - sincere, artistic, and inspirational. Still he would beat me unmercifully, game after game, day after day, week after week. Always with a smile, but not a drop of mercy: "*You'll win when you get tired of losing*", he would laughingly growl. Hmmm.

Meanwhile, I could only observe and assimilate, try on what I thought I'd learned. If I had an easy shot, and gave it a good whack for emphasis, he would cringe and bellow in that gargling voice, "*Samson was a lousy pool shooter!*" (*Explaining later that, "Samson died from being a little too enthusiastic."*) Then laugh uproariously at his Biblical joke, and my attempt to assert a power I had not yet learned to control. He would then, very gently, without one hard hit, "run the table", putting in all his balls and then mine, just for emphasis.

He was showing me, without speaking a word, that this could be done perfectly, without force or hullabaloo, simply by staying calm and visualizing what you wanted to happen and acting accordingly.

And we would move on. Lesson taught, and hopefully learned. Time was of the essence to Charlie. There was a lot to share and, as we both knew only too well, life could be cruelly and quite unexpectedly, short. I told him he should write a book for those who came after him. He looked me right in the eye, and quietly replied that the important things in life are only learned by doing. *"A book can describe a path for you, but no learning is going to happen 'til you start walking."*

Still, I got to assuage my mental/emotional pain somewhat with cheap beer, and, I had something new to think about. Something creative, that was also intensely personal. And it would one day make me a stronger and better person, long after the last ball had dropped.

When I finally won a game from him and asked if he had taken it easy on me, he indignantly growled back at me: "If I let you win, you didn't win! And if you cheated when I wasn't looking, you're already lost." Not, you *have* lost, mind you – you *are* lost. A distinction I noted. Thus was I prepared for the path to "higher and deeper realities."

The alcohol anesthetized the pain (and the ego) so that some deeper sense of self might be more accessible, should I aspire to such things. (Later, the alcohol would merely get in the way. Meditation, to be sure, was easier and cheaper - and there is no hangover! But, I had never even heard the word "meditation" yet. Ignorance may be many things – but I sincerely doubt that "bliss" is one of them.) Hell, I didn't even know what I was looking *for*. But I could feel something beginning to knock quietly at my back door. So I tried my best to at least appear "normal", and fit in with whatever was happening around me. This was a well-meaning attempt to "not be a problem", that would almost always prove futile.

My values, such as they were even before the accident, were by now totally out of harmony with what everyone else seemed to agree was the "real world". That was never more apparent than the day some poor soul from the *New York Life* insurance company, canvassing our neighborhood, came to my door only a few weeks after Doris' death.

He began by explaining how his company long ago had the dubious distinction of insuring almost everyone in the 7th Cavalry - on the day of the Little Big Horn massacre! (True story.) He opined, sadly, "That was a really bad day for the company." I said I thought we could all agree on that. So we talked, he trying to bridge the space between us, me just trying to relate to a nice normal guy attempting to sell me "life insurance", while I was in the middle of my own "what is life?" nightmare.

That soon after Doris' death, I was actually enjoying the rather bizarre company of someone whose entire industry was predicated on, literally, gambling on the projected demise of their customer base. Especially when he enthusiastically offered that, "with just a small investment every month" I, too, could be protected from "...*any eventuality that might somehow tragically occur, suddenly leaving loved ones helpless in its wake.*" (That was a great phrase, one I never forgot, since it seemed to describe life exactly as I had come to know it!) Plus, he added, again enthusiastically, in a mere twenty years I would have a tidy little nest egg that I could do *anything* with! That was where our perceptions of life diverged.

After a pause, looking straight into his eyes with all the kindness I could muster, and the conviction only experiential knowledge can give one, I gently informed his still grinning and relentlessly positive self that I happened to know, "for a fact", that he really had no idea what his life might look like "twenty *minutes* from now". He laughed, at first, and then looked confused. As we continued staring into each other it slowly occurred to him that I was utterly serious.

So I began to, as gently as possible, describe to him what a "really bad day" could look like, that was not just part of a historical actuary table. And why, at least from my admittedly personal point of view, he was a little late to that party. After a few minutes of sincere apologies, as each of us tried to comfort the other about the obvious vicissitudes of life, we shook hands warmly and he left to go home and be with his family - and to cherish anew his suddenly "pretty darn wonderful life".

Looking back, that appeared to be my first day at my new job, though that would not become apparent for some time to come. My search for understanding began in earnest. Over the next decade, there would be a lot of missteps and "wrong" paths, almost all of them due to two virtually universal conditions: First: Family interpretations and identities imposed on us all, very early in our lives, determining who we are and what we should be about with our lives.

Second: Culturally reinforced <u>ignorance</u> about who we *really* are, and what it is we should truly be about. It's a kind of double-barreled stupid-attack on our true nature that no one, save for a few iconoclasts out on the fringes of "acceptable" society, seemed to even acknowledge - let alone seek a cure for - and I certainly didn't know any of "them". Yet...

After Charlie's somewhat bizarre tutelage (and a brief word from the insurance companies of America) the world didn't seem quite so intimidating. I would embark on my life-long search for understanding, firmly embedded in the "now" of life. I harbored no illusions about the ephemeral quality of plans and dreams for some illusory future.

The first time I heard someone say, "Man plans, God laughs", I laughed right out loud –

apparently, right along with God. Somewhere inside of me, those four words struck a chord – and not only because of my experiences, but because deep in our Souls we really do <u>know</u>.

Intuitively, as essentially spiritual beings, we all suspect we were born for a reason. Long after we finally gain some semblance of personal success or comfort, there comes this feeling that *we should be "doing something"*. And if you live long enough you begin to see that any plan by our egos that is out of harmony with that "something" will never bring satisfaction - no matter how successful one might appear to be at any given moment.

I had absolutely no idea what that something might be. And, since I had no remaining connection to whoever I *had* been, or had ever even imagined I might become, I also had no idea about what might bring me happiness, or even begin to constitute success. At 21 years of age, I was legally a genuine adult. But I was also a blank slate – what some might call a "cipher". I was an intelligent and articulate, legal-to-do-anything, newborn babe. And I was wide open, ready and willing to go anywhere and do anything that might uncover even a clue about how and why some things happened to people.

My concerns were decidedly <u>not</u> about building a nest-egg for tomorrow – not even what I was going to eat later. No, I embraced each moment as it unfolded, all in the hope that it might provide even a hint about, *How did we get here? And, what the hell are the real rules?*

Those are two good and valid questions for anyone, at any time. Apparently, though, barring personal catastrophic trauma or some other tragedy, such questions are studiously avoided by "normal" people. Well, I had already followed the hand-me-down rules everyone already agreed upon since I was born – almost to the letter! That had not worked out well at all. Adding salt to my psychic wound was my religious upbringing. In the face of prolonged and excruciating pain and confusion, one cannot help but suspect that one might be being punished – but for what? Well, God only knew, and He wasn't talking.

The *"slings and arrows of outrageous fortune"* may sound profound, but it is cold comfort on a dark night alone, and not really a reason. My life was not a morality play or an inspirational movie, not even to me (yet)! It definitely was "harsh reality" – with an emphasis on the harsh.

Things don't just randomly happen, do they? We humans *do* have "free will". Within the parameters of what we are taught is acceptable behavior, we can choose to do, or not do, anything. In nature a "random" Fox may *appear* to happen upon a "random" Rabbit, but their actions – indeed, everything about them - is <u>obviously</u> part of a plan. A really BIG plan! Their ancestors have been doing this virtually forever - all in perfect harmony! *Something* is up, yes?

For the longest time, I did not realize that my search for a deeper understanding of Life was not one that everyone shared. Thus I was often profoundly embarrassed when I would joyously and enthusiastically attempt to share some monumental (to me!) discovery of the actual workings of our lives. I rushed to share my newfound "clue" with my friends, and the world. Surely, *everyone* would want to know this!

Not true.

Thankfully, while commiserating with the World Religions professor at *College Misericordia,* an all-girls (at the time) Catholic college just outside of Wilkes-Barre, I received a very important gift from him - the understanding that: "If you give 'The Answer' to someone who does not have 'the question', it's just gibberish - to them."

Well, that explained a great deal! Obviously, I would need to begin to seek out others with like concerns.

I didn't know it then, but throughout this "dark night" I was constantly being guided from within. And because I had no personal agenda, beyond finding the apparently unknowable "why", I had little or no reason to question my immediate impulse on anything, and thus was pretty close to hearing the "Divine" already. I just didn't know it.

I was already being prepared for, and guided toward, a future I could never have imagined, or probably even comprehended at the time. One thing I did know, even then, was that I *had* to somehow find people who knew, or at least wanted to know, the answers to the questions burning in my heart.

But, did such people even exist?

When the unemployment compensation ran out I figured I had better find a job. It would have been very easy to just surrender to the darkness. To become one of those guys you see sleeping in doorways after negotiating some way to stay numb that day.

I would supplement my search for some kind of understanding by doing menial jobs strictly for survival, a "career" was not even an idea I could entertain let alone follow through on. Outside of the obvious, such as male and human, I still had no concept of whom or what I was. And I had nary a clue about what, if anything, could be done about that.

I felt like an alien among 'normal' people. Other people had 'real' concerns, 'real' lives. I actually envied anyone who mindlessly went to what even they admitted was a "mindless" job every day, never once thinking that mind-blowing soul-searing madness might be just around the next corner.

Maybe they did, but they weren't going to spend a great deal of time thinking about it.

Everyone else seemed to have 'real' things to think about. I looked at the same world they did, and I couldn't think of it any other way: What the hell is going on here? What is it we are all doing? Is there a purpose to life? How, and why, do things happen?

Unfortunately for me, those questions never seemed to bother anyone else I knew. Wandering the streets, bars, and night-clubs of Wilkes-Barre and environs, trying to find "something", I was eventually introduced to the kind of a "shady" world I'd only experienced in the movies of the 40's and 50's. But, the denizens of this world were apparently just what I needed.

Jesse Wade, was the pianist in a 5 piece all black jazz combo: Piano, Bass, Sax and Drums, and "Choo-choo" Coleman on vocals. They were all in their 50's or 60's, except for the diminutive "Ol' Pete" on giant stand-up Bass, who seemed to be nearing a hundred (and might weigh almost that much), and "the kid" on Sax, who appeared to be about 40.

Jesse was very soft spoken, the kindest, gentlest man of any size or color I had ever met. He played piano in the styles of Errol Garner and Oscar Peterson (with a touch of Thelonius), all his idols. He was, just like old Charlie was at pool, world-class good and virtually invisible in a small city in the Pocono Mountains - a "victim of circumstance", if ever there was such a thing.

I learned something very important about the nature of 'reality', being with both of these men virtually back-to-back: Just because the lightning bolt of fame doesn't strike you, doesn't mean you are not worthy of it. In my life I would eventually meet more than a few people deserving of at least national recognition, most of whom would never get it, and yet they filled the world with their beauty and grace, inspiring and lifting everyone they touched.

Jesse and the group played in the nightclubs on the "bad" side of town, where I had gravitated in an attempt to expand my world beyond Hell - and Charlie's. It was a racially mixed crowd, but I still stuck out like a compound fracture, a 21 year-old, lily-white, fresh-faced drunken innocent, who appeared to have stumbled into, or out of, some dark *Damon Runyon* tragicomedy.

I describe it that way because of the "atmosphere" of the places I was being drawn to. To those of us born and raised there, it was understood that, at least culturally, "everything gets to Wilkes-Barre twenty years later". So by 1964, the forties actually were the cultural time frame. This was not a bad thing! The bars and nightclubs in that part of town, almost without exception, were at least twenty or more years old (some much more). There was interesting and often great architecture inside and out. In terms of atmosphere and the inhabitants, it appeared my personal mystery/nightmare was going *film noir!* God was *The Maltese Falcon,* and the set was *Casablanca* west.

Into the midst of all this came I, just wanting to let the music and alcohol fill my mind until there was no space for memories, no matter how recent. In the middle of the band's second set, the drummer had an attack of appendicitis and was taken away in an ambulance. By that time, I was just drunk enough to volunteer to sit in if they would "just keep it simple, some swing and ballads" (and the crowd was just drunk enough to enthusiastically welcome me), and after a song or two, we got in a groove.

Co-creating music of that kind demands the kind of inner focus that transcends even the alcohol, at least if you're doing it right. I gratefully surrendered my thought processes, and focused all my attention on quickly learning the strange "kit" as well as the music.

At the end of that first night, the band stayed around "after hours", as was usual. We took some time to share our stories and they asked me to come back, at least for the next night, as there was no guarantee they'd see the other guy for a while. Much later, very early morning actually, Jesse took me home with him to sleep (pass out) on the family couch. Of course, he lived on the "wrong" side of town - it was 1964, and there definitely was such a thing. Even up north in Pennsylvania. As he helped me to his couch that first night, my head spinning, he whispered softly in my ear, "Relax, young brother, you're among friends. Folks 'round here know a little 'bout the blues." I was most assuredly very relaxed.

When I awoke I found he had a gaggle of kids, a warm and gracious wife - and gin in his breakfast coffee! Coffee recipe notwithstanding, he also played the organ in church every Sunday, "religiously".

I don't remember why (aside from some more of God's inscrutable will), but the drummer never did come back and I ended up buying the guy's drums and playing steadily with the band. When we couldn't book the whole combo, Jesse and I would play as a duo called "Salt & Pepper", that way we could play some of the same clubs during the week when the crowd wasn't as big. It was surely not what any doctor, counselor or priest would have recommended - but it saved my life, no doubt.

(That was 1964. How different is life today? I went home a while back [2009] and found that "old Jesse" now lived alone in an apartment in a low income project. I was thrilled beyond words just to know he was still alive. That alone was miraculous. According to my source, he was also still playing(!), but only in church on Sundays. I was able to find the right building, but none of the young people outside would tell me in which apartment he lived - I was a white guy in 'nice' clothes driving a white Dodge Caravan! The few hanging out whom I tried to speak with were all trying hard to look like they were already deep in the "thug life", and you didn't have to be Edgar Cayce to know what they were thinking. I had tears in my eyes when I finally gave up and had to drive away. Not knowing when I might return to my old hometown, I was pretty sure Jesse would be gone by the time that ever happened again. It still hurts.)

During that time of playing with Jesse I also began to gig with other musicians, doing any kind of music with anyone who needed a drummer. I was easing back into the world again, and being a musician enabled me to be, "*in the world but not of it*". It also helped keep me as sane as I was probably going to get any time soon.

Doing random gigs with some young people in a Rock & Roll band - early Beatles, Kinks, Stones, etc. - I had only one physical encounter of the intimate kind, with a beautiful young woman who was the on-again off-again girlfriend of the bass player. It was some months after Doris' death, and I managed to impregnate the young lady who I'm sure, at least at the time, was merely being compassionate toward the obviously wounded, semi-anesthetized drummer. As a result of this we entered into a marriage that probably should never have happened - except that it would serve as the vehicle for the creation of our two beautiful children, who simply had the bad luck to be born to a virtually "certifiable" father.

It was what we called a "shotgun" wedding in those times. But it was also another one of those improbable occurrences, engineered from above and beyond, that contributed to the saving of my life. When it happened, I was not on a road that led anywhere good. I was living my life in a way that pretty much guaranteed it would not last very long, and that was more than all right with me. Drinking myself to death was not like "real" suicide, it was merely a side benefit! God and I would work it out later.

Ours was not a romantic love, as we barely knew each other, but we did manage to create another child while also struggling mightily through the motions of an actual marriage. That was primarily because I was still walking around in what appeared to be a confusing dream (it was less than a year since Doris' death), and nothing still seemed quite "real" to me. The marriage was destined for disaster, simply because I was the worst possible choice for a mate anyone should ever be saddled with. Even though it was not a serious romantic union, we were devoted parents for as long as it lasted. Afterward, it would take decades for our two children to forgive me for the virtually inevitable break-up of their home.

Clinically, I was mentally unstable and emotionally disconnected, and I had no business even pretending I could be responsible for, or to, anyone else. But there we were.

Trying to get back into some kind of "reality" based life, for my pregnant wife and coming child, I left Wilkes-Barre for Washington, DC to join the Metropolitan Police Force. Police-work was the only formal training or schooling I had beyond High School. They had a poster at the unemployment office offering 20 grand a year to start, a princely sum in 1965, especially for a guy from an already officially declared "depressed area". While I waited for the police academy to open up, I took a job in sales at an auto parts store/speed shop called *Hi-Gear Tire and Auto*, and soon discovered that I was very good at "sales" and organizing things. [Capricorn w/Cancer Moon and Pisces rising - I would come to understand the implications of all that much later.]

My success stemmed from the fact that I genuinely cared for the people who came in the store and they felt that, and trusted me. I never abused that trust and always steered them toward only the best of what they needed and could afford. They "got" that, and I and the company prospered. The company grew from 5 stores to nearly twenty in the time after I joined them, and I saw no reason to leave and return to police work.

When Martin Luther King was assassinated, and a good chunk of our nation's capitol was going up in flames, my wife informed me that she would not even attempt to raise children in such an environment, although we actually lived in the suburbs of Maryland a few miles across the city line. So we packed up a U-Haul and I drove a truck full of our "stuff" back to the Wyoming Valley of Pennsylvania.

There were only a few decent jobs in our area that were even remotely similar to what I had been doing. And, even when I would find one, fate still kept intervening in ways that I can now look back on and see were clearly designed to get me out of any life-stream that would prevent my discovering my Soul's purpose.

And "away" we go!

One day, while out trying to find yet another job, I came upon a strange looking little store-front. The large windows and the glass door were completely covered from the inside with *Mylar,* giving them the appearance of distorted mirrors, real Fun House quality reflections. It was called, *"The Ultra Inn".* It was a "Head Shop" – and I had never even heard of such a thing.

Upon entering, out of sheer curiosity, I beheld a statuesque blonde woman (a former New York model!) dressed in a modest but elegant black dress standing behind the cash register. She was smiling and had just blown out a black candle perched atop the old ornate cash-register. She said she was the store's owner and had originally opened it as a "Black & White Boutique", just like the one she also owned in New York's Greenwich Village. Along with the clothing, she stocked an assortment of *Hookahs, "Bongs"* and other smoking pipes, as well as rolling papers, posters, Ultra-violet lights, strobe lights, candles and incense, and an assortment of "Hippy" and "counter-culture" clothing and other paraphernalia. Very cool and urbane in New York's "Village" - but a brand-spanking-new idea, in little old Wilkes-Barre, PA!

She introduced herself as "Keri" and offered that she had just completed a prayer and candle-burning ceremony, asking Spirit to bring her someone she could trust to run the store in her absence, so she could pay more attention to her life in New York. The previous "managers", a couple in their late twenties who lived upstairs, were leaving to go live in a Yoga Ashram. After "what's your name?" came, "what is your birthday?" And we discovered that we shared the same, rather auspicious, birthday - Christmas Eve. She decided right then and there that I would be perfect for the new manager's position, as I had obviously been divinely guided to her store. This was my first clue that there seemed to be a purpose (perhaps even a science?) to life - beyond survival in it. And, that certain people even had some understanding of how "It" worked!

While we were personally never more than spiritual business partners, concerned simply with the running of her store (she resided in NY and sent me new merchandise every week), her trust in me had placed me where I would soon meet plenty of others who were also curious about the nature and meaning of life. I would quickly be exposed to wonderful new ideas and understandings, enlightened and enlightening philosophical discussions, as well as yoga, vegetarianism and, of course, altered states of consciousness.

I was so excited to meet these people, I even brought some of my new acquaintances home for dinner to meet my wife and family! There was Paul Wright, professorially bearded Insurance executive, who wore expensive suits and drove a silver Chrysler Imperial convertible and *loved* Bob Dylan, The Doors,

The Moody Blues - and LSD! (Paul eventually left his corporate position to be a Psychiatric Nurse in a mental hospital); Richard Wade, a "Black Panther" Martial Arts *Sensei*; a young brother/sister couple named Raymond and Amber, who seemed to know a lot more about what I wanted to learn than most of the spiritual teachers I had been able to find.

I was (even in my obviously battered soul) very much like all of them. Suffice to say, my wife was not, and it was not long before my marriage painfully dissolved and I became a full-fledged, 'tie-dyed'-in-the-wool, hippy. But, not just any old hippy! Oh, no.

I, who had never even seen a "joint", or anything else that we sold in the store, was now the manager of Wilkes-Barre's only "Head Shop" - *located directly across the street from City Hall!* I was no stranger to that place.

My uncle, and former back-yard-neighbor in the old neighborhood, was by then the senior (day shift) Desk-Sergeant of the Wilkes-Barre Police Force, and my father was a very well known and respected Television announcer, as well as the much loved and most sought after Master-of-Ceremonies at all the important, and official, city/social functions. All of this merely confirmed my suspicions that "Something" was setting this all up. But, why me? And, for what? God only knew - and I was still trying hard to get my hands on Him.

In the midst of this confluence of circumstances, I was soon the talk of the town - and did not even know it, as I did not travel with my father's crowd: *"That's Jim's son. You know, the one who's wife was killed? He's running that hippy joint across the street. Poor guy, he's really lost his mind."*

This only confirmed what I was reluctantly beginning to suspect - that I was probably never going to be like other people, no matter how hard I tried. Because of my empathy, and sympathy for the suffering of others which my own pain had awakened within me, I seemed destined to spend a great deal of my time on earth trying to explain to "normal" people why those "other" people are the way they are - and how they probably got that way. Still, no matter how hard I personally tried to actually *be* normal, it was obviously not going to be, at least in this lifetime. But, I was learning how to just say "Oh, well" or "Now what?", and contentedly, if not joyfully mean it. Forty years later, the "screensaver" on my lap-top is the phrase, *"Now what!"* slowly tumbling and spinning across a background of stars and galaxies!

I relate all this simply to help readers understand just how fragile our sense of identity is. Most of all, I hope everyone comes to recognize how my personal experiences actually reflect the nature of *every* human life, with just varying degrees of intensity. After a few painful experiences, we all begin to question our lives – and hopefully, begin to discern the pattern.

Who am I? What should I be doing with my life? What would I like to be doing with my life? These are not light ponderings, and they are not always answerable in simple day-to-day life. If they were, there would never have been a need for rabbis, priests, ministers, spiritual teachers, prophets, psychics, spiritual readings, etc. In Proverbs 4:7 we are enjoined: "In all thine getting, my child, get understanding." . . . easier said than done.

It is difficult to comprehend, from the ego level alone that, while we are all experiencing apparently wildly divergent lives and situations, we are all also learning the very same "Soul" lessons from them. And those lessons will eventually lead to our completely natural oneness with Creation itself. On the way, we will all reap what we have sown. And in the reaping, we will become healed in our souls of the selfishness that is at the heart of all our suffering.

Almost predictably, given the nature of our coming together, my wife and I reached a crisis point in our relationship. Both of us unhappy, confused, lacking any kind of guidance from within or without, we were quietly but irrevocably chipping away at whatever peaceful coexistence we had established, in our ignorance and inexperience.

At my "job" in the head-shop, most people came and went quickly. But there were a few of those aforementioned "iconoclasts out on the fringes of society", that I was now meeting, who liked to 'hang out' and just talk, play a game of chess or three while listening to the music, etc. The young girl, Amber, and I had what I know understand as a serious Karmic connection. She came by the store almost every day and often didn't leave until shortly before closing. Most of the time, she was in the company of her somewhat older brother. They were both free and open-minded in a way that I had never been at their age. I thought they were in college because of their demeanor and extensive knowledge of things I didn't even know existed.

The feeling that existed between us was so strong that I had to tell my wife about it. Our own relationship had at least begun like that, though the responsibilities of parenthood and jobs, etc., had taken its toll, as it does for all couples with children.

We began with an honest appraisal of our relationship that evolved into a soul-baring. There were true and heartfelt confessions, tears, apologies and forgiveness leading to the realization of what we had evolved into as a couple and a family, and a deep abiding commitment to love and honor each other and our children. She asked that I tell Amber that she could no longer come to the store and just hang out all day. And I gladly promised I would, the very next time I saw her.

The next day, upon her arrival, I put the "Waaay out to lunch!" sign on the door and asked her to join me on Public Square, two blocks away. We sat on a bench as I explained what had transpired with my wife and I and how our commitment to providing a stable and loving home for our children had to take precedence over every other consideration in our lives. It was why we had returned to Wilkes-Barre, even though I left a position in my cousin's business that would have made us very wealthy. I told her she could continue to shop there, but could no longer spend the afternoon just hanging out there.

Though we had never so much as even touched each other, she was crying but said she understood. As we walked back to the store, she said this would be the last time I saw her as it would be too painful, she had come to really love me and could not be in my presence. I said I was thankful that she understood, and I would accept that we wouldn't see each other again. She asked if she could hold my hand just once, as we walked what was left of the two blocks. I said, "sure". And that's when *karma*, in the form of my wife, walked around the corner, and all hell broke loose – in public, on a crowded sidewalk, on an otherwise sunny day.

As we approached each other, she gave no hint at what she was feeling about what she saw. I was exhibiting what I thought was a reassuring smile. When we came together, almost directly in front of the store, she exploded! Hitting me and screaming at the top of her voice, horrible things that only someone who feels absolutely betrayed can muster, while I kept repeating, "It's alright! I did what you asked. She is just saying goodbye. I love you. We're alright. Everything's fine. Please stop, and listen!"

She was hysterical, not able to even hear me above her pain and screaming.

After what was probably less than a minute, but seemed an eternity, she spun around, and ran up the street and back around the same corner she appeared from. Amber was gone. It would be many days before I ever saw her or her brother again.

I knew I had to give her time to calm down, so I stayed at the store a few more hours. I closed early and went home to explain the circumstances, illuminate the misunderstanding, so we could all begin our lives anew.

When I arrived home, I found all my clothes and belongings; Bowling ball; Baseball glove and spikes; Frisbees, et al, in large plastic bags on the front porch – with a note. She would never speak to me again, ever! She had changed the locks and was leaving with the kids and would not say where they would be or when they would return. I was stunned, in great confusion and pain. My kids were my life!

I got a room at the YMCA and over the days and weeks proceeded to call relentlessly to explain. The moment she heard my voice, she would yell some invective and or threat, and slam the phone down. I wrote a multi-page letter explaining in detail what had transpired, professing my love and devotion to her and our family, and personally deposited it in our mailbox one evening.

The next day, I called expecting an "Oh, honey, I'm so sorry! I had no idea!"

Instead, I got: *"I found your letter in the mailbox and burned it without opening it! I said I never, ever want to hear from you again! Ever!"* and hung up.

I began to approach her after her job, in front of Pomeroy's Department Store on Public Square where she worked. Upon seeing me, she would scream, "Get away from me! I'll call the Police!" To this day, May of 2012 as I write this, she has never communicated with me in *any* way!

What is most noteworthy about this all is, some years later, upon my settling down in Virginia Beach, I was directed to a gifted woman locally acknowledged as a true "psychic", in a town that knows more than a little about such things.

In the "reading" I scheduled with her, without us having ever met or conversed about anything anywhere, beyond my name and birth date a few minutes before, she went into a semi-trance state and proceeded to describe how, in a lifetime as Native Americans in which I was a "Medicine Man", my wife of this time had "stolen" me from the young girl I was involved with in this time (Amber), and now, even though it was not real to anyone else, she believed that what she saw was real, and a betrayal, and was made by her own thoughts and feeling to experience the very same pain, confusion and emotions that she had caused another (Amber) to experience. There was <u>nothing</u> real about the little vignette we enacted on that sidewalk, but her feelings. Yet the lives of us all were irreparably changed in that moment. By Karma.

Unfortunately, back in Wilkes-Barre, my wife had initiated a relationship with a neighbor, probably the one she confessed having feelings for in our catharsis night, and had moved in with him with our kids. I, by now being a full-fledged hippy (read: social outcast!) was advised by my own father and the rest of my family to, "Leave the kids alone. You'll only cause confusion in their parental authority, and undermine "Earl's" chance to be a father-figure to them. He's a really good hard-working guy who owns his own gas-station, and the kids like him a lot." Our kids were only 3 and 2 at the time, but I was really close to them, until then.

Most of what I was told was not true. Every night, as I stared at the ceiling in that YMCA, my heart was being ripped apart. I could not believe such a loss could be happening to me again. It was not until they were teenagers that I would see my daughter and find out the truth. Earl was not a nice guy. They would lie awake at night and my daughter would console my son with tales about how their "real Dad" was going to come and rescue them, and take them away. They are still mad at me for not being there for them, even after we have all grown. Hence the idea of actual "Karma" lasting for centuries, until it is reconciled and balanced, for Love's sake alone. Life goes on, forever, and we will all have ample opportunity to "fix" everything!

"Those damn hippies!"

One experience in that time illustrates this perfectly. To this day it informs my interactions with the myriad "other" people who inhabit this world. This singular occurrence illuminated (or dispelled) any illusions I had about race, gender, socio-economic status, religion, political beliefs, loyalties, egos – *everything we use to allow ourselves to become comfortable in our separateness!* It would be a brief preview of my coming experience with The Light itself. But just a preview because, at the time, I was not yet ready to completely open my mind or heart to that which I found too alien, too 'different', to embrace.

I had a very close friend who, at least at that time in the early to mid seventies, was virtually the embodiment of everything different from me - the aforementioned Richard Wade. Richard, was 6 feet 4 inches tall and a nice medium brown, with an "afro" that would have made Angela Davis proud. We didn't really have any "black radicals" in little Wilkes-Barre, Pa., but Richard was such an imposing physical figure that he created the illusion of just such a "threat" merely by his presence - except that, once he spoke, you knew he was very much in love with <u>all</u> the life around him, including you.

He was prone to wearing a bright colorful form of African clothing called a *Dashiki,* and often a full length African ceremonial robe. He was a *Sensei,* a black-belt *Martial Arts* instructor, who was an expert with *Nunchucks*, and his constant companion was a huge slobbering friendly St. Bernard named "Bear".

Richard also played a pretty fine self-taught flute, a wicked game of chess, and despite his intimidating and regal appearance, he was as child-like a man as you will ever find in a grown-up's body.

While he could quite naturally *be* the role his appearance seemed to project into the world - strong, taciturn, graceful, every inch of African royalty - he was also the funniest, most spontaneously goofy of us all. And that is really saying something, since finding the apparently elusive "happiness" (elusive at least to our parents and most of our elders) was exactly what we were all about. We were counter-culture clowns, dedicated to unearthing the joy in every day - and if it wasn't there, creating it!

We were decidedly *not* the media-creation "dirty hippy" sex and drug addled misfits. Oh, no. We were very serious mind-expanding, soul-searching, God-loving, Jesus and Saint Francis emulating, harbingers of the second-coming! The vanguard of the New Age of spiritually realized humans who were *already* living as the brotherhood of man!

The picture inserted on the following page was prompted by an episode of simple human kindness (not at all "random" in our world), and the strange sense of "personal responsibility" that inspired many of us to live our lives the way we did. One of the early "motivational" truths I learned was, "If you see a job that needs doing, and nobody else even sees it – well, guess whose job it is?

The Author

From The Times-Leader Evening News (1973)

Above the heads of the stick figures holding hands and encircling the balloon, is the *Beatles* phrase and song title:

"...all you need is love is all you need is love is all you need is love is all you need..."

One fine summer day on Public Square (in the background of the photo) two "little-old-ladies" were sitting peacefully on one of the elaborate wood and wrought-iron bench swings left over from the turn of the century, quietly enjoying the afternoon sun. With each forward movement the swing made a pretty loud squeaking sound, nothing too obnoxious, unless you were the one sitting on it. I decided to walk across the street to a "5 &10-cent Store" and spend 29 cents on a can of "3-in-1" oil. When I got back, the ladies were still gently swinging to the squeak of the rusty hinge on top. I quietly came up behind them and applied a drop or two of oil to each of the hinges, and *presto!* As we used to joke: "Peace broke out."

The ladies, surprised by the sudden silencing of the noise, turned and saw me. They both smiled and effusively offered their heart-felt thanks. Then, with a laugh, one said, "It's the little things, isn't it?" Amen, sisters.

Well, it seems the ladies were so moved by the fact that someone would do such a thing - and, that "someone like me" was not at all like they expected someone like me to be - they must have called the local newspaper to report this early "random act of kindness". The paper immediately sent a reporter and a photographer to find me on Public Square, and the very next day there I was - on the front page of the "Local Section" of our daily newspaper! - explaining myself, my friends, and our motivations, to the world. (This was especially noteworthy because just a few weeks before, a *Letter to the Editor* in the same paper complained about the "Hippie-types" gathering on Public Square "jostling" innocent shoppers and by-standers! This inspired a handful of us to immediately create and have printed up, some genuine *"Ultra-Inn Jostling Team"* T-shirts, hopefully giving us some kind of comic credibility.)

Anyway, I informed the reporter that I was already 31 years old (this was *"Never trust anyone over 30!"* time), and suggested that perhaps I might represent an adult, maybe even a father figure, the kids could actually relate to, since most of the local "hippy" faction were just high-school or college kids with a couple of 'Nam vets thrown in. Most parents in Wilkes-Barre and its environs (and the rest of the world!) were just not able to talk to their kids about what was happening to them, and around them.

Thus was born my very first public persona, complete with photo-op! The caption read: "Father Hippy". Strange days, indeed.

One day, in the midst of this wondrous time, his royal high-ness Richard and I ended up at my home while everyone else was out, and he "just happened to have" two capsules of *psilocybin*, a very potent extract from the *Psilocybin* ("magic") mushroom family.

At that time of our lives, it was considered one of God's greatest gifts to mankind. An actual religious Sacrament in the Southwestern Native American traditions, it is designed by Nature Herself to open the human brain-mind to the higher realms of Spirit. Of course, many outside the Native American culture are also inclined to such spiritually motivated seeking . . . . . really!

Richard also brought with him an LP of a Jazz "fusion" group that was touring the world named *Osibisa,* made up of four African and three Caribbean musicians, that he desperately wanted me to hear. Richard was aware of my musical background, we had often "jammed" together when some type of percussion instrument was available, and he was sure I would *love* it!

He had long been a regular guest at our home where I would often play *my* music for him: Moody Blues, Pink Floyd, Cat Stevens, CSNY, etc., all groundbreaking, at that time, but, as he said, we heard them all the time, some even on the radio, and *Osibisa* would be new and enlightening for me.

So we prayed our thanks to the Great Spirit, asking for His/Her blessings and protection, partook of the sacrament, and relaxed and meditated for a while. Soon enough, the physical and visual sensations began as the glands of the endocrine system - the *chakras* - began to open. We decided we had better put on the music while we still could. LP's were large black vinyl discs with a tiny hole in the center, through which an even tinier spindle in the center of a spinning turntable was to be inserted - already, that simple act had assumed the magnitude of a daunting task!

Recognizing that this might be the last opportunity to take advantage of physical mobility I went to the kitchen and got us something to drink. By the time I got back, Richard had gotten the album onto the turntable and was watching it spin, waiting to lower the playing arm onto the disk and grinning from ear to ear. It was obviously time for us to set our bodies down.

Now, the principle determining factors that govern any experience of mind expansion are "set" and "setting". *Set*, is your own mind-set, what you believe is going to happen, your expectations of the coming experience; *Setting*, is the atmosphere in which the experience is going to take place.

Looking back, I understand that I had the "*set*" of expecting a pleasurable and enlightening experience in the comfort of the "*setting*" of the familiar and comfortable surroundings of my home. So when Richard lowered the needle onto the album we both leaned back and opened ourselves to the music. It began with a trumpet scatting all up and down the scale along with some kind of free-form cacophony of African bells and steel-drums playing disjointed poly-rhythms that didn't "make any sense" to my western-music educated ear. It didn't take long for me to get really uncomfortable because my expectations were of an entirely different musical and emotional space.

In my mind set, the activity we had embarked on was of the more subtle, gentle, easing on into the inner peace mode. I could not associate the sounds I was hearing with anything remotely like that. I asked Richard to please stop it, so we could talk about it. When I expressed my surprise and described what it felt like to me, he just smiled and said "You're not listening, man" -- and started it again!

This time I sat back and closed my eyes, and off we went again. I listened to as much as I could, but it actually became emotionally painful. It sounded dark and chaotic, alien - and *very* uncomfortable. I asked him to please stop it, again, which he did. I said it was painful to me, that it sounded almost "evil".

He looked right in my eyes, without a smile, and said, "You are not listening, *brothuh.*" Waited a long moment, looking at me - and started it again!

This time I sat back, and, like an actual musician should, I listened without judgment. I closed my eyes, emptied my mind, and surrendered to the sounds. Trying to "see" the music within me, find the message, wanting to at least appreciate the expertise of the players, no matter what the music.

African bells, Caribbean chimes and steel-drums, atonal trumpet meanderings up, down, around and through any scale I was familiar with, it was a dissonant jarring collection of sounds that was simply foreign to me, especially as music! I began to fear that this was going to be my "freak-out" experience, and hoped there would be enough of "me" left to put back together, when the sounds began to merge into a pattern, a pulse I could recognize, and then . . . wait . . . what's that?

Voices, slowly becoming audible through the music, dimly in the background, singing a kind of chant. Words, just barely perceptible. Listening, listening deeper, as they became more discernable...

"We,

Through the Spirit of our ancestors,

Bring you love.

Our precious gift, of happiness!

Forget your problems, see beyond.

And, love!

And be happy!

Ah! Be happy!"

There was Richard, still not smiling, silent, eyes like doorways, completely open to me – now we were looking *into* each other, not at each other, our minds quiet and receptive, melding into one another, becoming One. We saw, acknowledging silently and simultaneously, our Oneness from some long ago beginning that was also . . . *right now!*

Our particularized points of awareness flying through time and memory, showing, like two movies running at the same time into and around each other, how every experience of our individual lives, wildly dissimilar in cultural and physical expression, had taught us each the *exact* same lessons – and informed every choice we had made, from "The Beginning" right up to that day and moment, had brought us to *that* room, at *that* time, under *those* circumstances - and that an entire chapter of Life, existence as parts of God's own wondrous journey through Creation, was completed the moment we became that Oneness with each other. We laughed and embraced and danced, with the subdued abandon and grace of two very 'high' humans who did not quite have complete control of their bodies – but their Spirits were in full flight!

Now, whenever we were ready, we could both walk out the door of that house, my worldly home, as one - as _The_ One - and the rest of the world was waiting, waiting for us to bring that awareness and joy, the joy of The Oneness of All Life, to it. Let the healing of the world commence!

> _"But trailing clouds of Glory do we_
> _come, from God who is our home."_
> ~ Wordsworth

In the course of a decade I would attempt to glean from every religion I could find, the God that they all purported to have access to. They were, of course, all as correct as they were inadequate. Mostly because, over the course of their existence, each had _become_ the God they had previously been worshipping. By now, obedience to the evolving rules of the belief system had replaced the original purpose – actual union with God.

Still, I found that each of them had a valuable gift for my Soul in its quest for its Source. For example: The 7 Sacraments of my Catholic upbringing, with extremely effective ritual and ceremony, marked the evolution of a human being's journey through this world; *Hatha* Yoga would teach me how to care for my body as a living temple of Spirit; *Bhakti* Yoga, the yoga of devotion; *Raja* Yoga, the yoga of the mind; Buddhism would teach me to discipline my thoughts, even as I disciplined my body and desires; Islam taught me, as did Judaism, that the worship of God in everyday matters could not be segregated to a specific weekly time period, but in the *living of a life.* A life that contained constant reminders that it is <u>always</u> in God that "...we live and move and have our being". And, that each day was fraught with possibilities, constant opportunities, to "walk your talk", especially by serving the less fortunate that God places before us all every day; Sufism taught me that the Holy Spirit of God Himself was actually a symphony, the unspeakably glorious Dance of Creation, and that I could experience my part in that manifestation at anytime, simply by singing and dancing with joyous abandon and God on my mind. In those moments, God and I were One!

On and on I searched and travelled, through every religion, belief system or "mystery school", I could find. To me they seemed as fingers on the hands of God - every one different, but truly useful only as parts of the whole.

"Yourself as a Soul, made of the breath of God, to be a companion with Him for eternity!"
E. Cayce Rdg

One fine day, a customer in the "Ultra Inn" who had overheard one of our many ongoing discussions about "Life, 'Liberation', and the Pursuit of Happiness", handed me a book entitled *Many Mansions*. It was a veritable banquet for a starving soul, and Life would never be the same again.

Dr. Gina Cerminara had been guided to investigate the "psychic" readings of Edgar Cayce, in Virginia Beach. In her education as a psychologist she had already studied many of the world's religions. Consequently she was familiar with the concept of reincarnation and karma, and the possibility of other life experiences in this world as an eternal soul. The Cayce material seemed to illuminate a prior cause for many phobias, congenital defects, and such that often have no plausible genesis in a patient or subject's present life.

After studying much of the Cayce material myself for over thirty years I can state that her book might be the most comprehensive, and also most easily comprehended, of the many books about and inspired by the Edgar Cayce readings. This is most certainly true in respect to the clinical understanding of the nature of the mind/soul, and the practical application of such information.

The root of the word Psychology is the word *Psyche*, meaning Soul, and she was the perfect Psychologist to see and interpret the significance of Cayce's work for medical and science professionals. She had a perfect balance of intellect and heart.

It was said of her that: *"...while she was a trained scientist, possessing a deeply curious and penetrating analytical mind, she expressed herself with the soul of a poet. No nuance of the human condition escaped her loving eye."* Perfectly described!

Just a few of the 25 chapters that make up the book are:

An answer to the riddle of life /A new dimension in Psychology / The Magnificent Possibility / Past-life origins of mental abnormalities /Marriage and the Destiny of Women / Infidelity and Divorce /Parents and Children / Implications of the data on human abilities /A philosophy to live by. And that's not even half of the chapter titles!

My God, who would *not* want to know these things? Understanding the true nature of one's own being, within the context of *those* very human and universal issues, and more?

(You would be surprised...)

Her book is filled with direct quotations from the actual "readings" of Edgar. This is information from the Soul's own record, beginning with our birth in the heart and mind of that which we call God.

This record, the *Akasha*, is also known as "The Book of Life", and is described by the apostle John in *The Book of the Revelation*. It is available within us all. It has been promised: *"I will bring to thine remembrance all things, whatsoever you have need of, from the beginning."*

But, more importantly, it was the way Dr. Cerminara clarified how the various neuroses, phobias, personal predilections, and the daily life choices of the subjects work <u>in all our lives.</u> It was her cogent analysis and uncomplicated articulation of complex psychological theory that focused the light of reason on the "Holy Grail" of my own long and painful search: "The Holy <u>*Why?*</u> " Not the precise cause. That would soon come, but in its time. Still, it was more than enough, at long last, to know that there *was* a reason. One that I could seek – and find!

I rejoiced in the knowledge that not only was it possible to *find* reason and truth, but "finding out His ways" was the actual purpose of our lives! Our Creator Source wants us to <u>know</u> - while we're here, not when we die! Wants us to understand - not just what, but the how and the why!

I had just been given the most valuable gift possible for me. The understanding that no matter how bizarre my life had been, there actually <u>was</u> a purpose - for *everything!* And, it was not only possible, but my personal responsibility, to discover <u>within me</u> all that I had been seeking!

The Cayce material is most noteworthy for its decidedly biblical theme and references, much of that no doubt due to Edgar's devout perusal of the Bible - every day and completely through, from Genesis to Revelations over the course of a year, for every year of his life!

This was important to me because, I had been raised a Catholic, and not encouraged to read The Bible, and I think I know why. Therein lie the words, "Call no man 'Father', your Father is in Heaven"; and, "Do not array yourself in fine robes, praying in public for others to see." Those phrases leaped off the pages to me, and were very difficult for me to reconcile with my "faith".

Truth be told, I don't recall even having a Bible in our home. Growing up, the only Bible I ever saw regularly was a huge ornate always-open tome, resting on an equally ornate gold-plated stand in the center of the great altar of our cathedral-like Roman Catholic Church. On Sundays, only the priest ever read from it! And usually ceremonially, while some young altar-boy struggling under the weight and bulk of both the book and stand was allowed to carry it across the altar to him, and back!

But you don't have to be a Bible Scholar to understand that the good Dr. Cerminara had uncovered the *Truth*, with a capitol 'T'. The biblical references not only gave a certain authority to their accuracy, as they were easily verifiable, but it was also perfectly logical! Whatever you cause another to experience, must one day become your experience. "Whatsoever a man soweth, that must he also reap." Perfect! I was not a big fan of the "...every jot and every tittle..." part, as that implied someone would one day think of me as I had thought of them, or even someone else; and someone would someday cause me to *feel* what I had caused another to feel. Oh, dear.

It would be some time before the "Grace of God" became more than words. The ego, for all its bluster and rationalizing, is still very much like a frightened child when confronted with responsibility for its actions. Evasion and avoidance, its survival tools, only keep it from the One Thing that will save it - the incomprehensible and all-encompassing *Love* of which we are made.

The Universal Spirit of God described in *Many Mansions* was a "beyond religion" perspective of the Living God: He (and/or She) is not constrained by the interpretations of Bible Scholars or spiritual teachers of any kind. The readings themselves present a comprehensive understanding of, and deep respect for, *all* religions across the record of human experience. Dr. Gina's coherent analyses make it all very relevant and immediate; absolutely real, and in the present tense. Nothing 'meta'-physical about it!

In no time at all, the Good Lord's famously "strange and mysterious ways" were beginning to appear far more "strange" than I could have ever imagined – and, at the same time, far less "mysterious" than I could have ever hoped. The whole concept of a God above, trying to get *into* our lives, is replaced by the _presence_ of God, inside of us all, trying to get out. Now *that* makes sense!

Finally, the admonition from the readings that, "You don't *have* a Soul, you <u>are</u> a Soul! What you 'have' is an identity problem", blew open the windows to *my* own soul! It was not just life-changing, though that should certainly be enough for anyone, but, far more importantly to me, it was life-<u>affirming</u>! The very perspective that had been missing from my own existence for a decade!

Up until that moment, I was still waiting to die to find out how and why my life was as it is. Now, I could begin to actually _live_ again, live my life as a Soul, a *spiritual* being, one that had entered this world to experience my own personal (and probably some group) *karma* – reap what I had sown amongst those with whom I had sown it, and *vice versa* - all simply in order to be inspired to seek and remember my own true nature. Upon which, if I applied due diligence, I would eventually meet God face-to-face! (And, no doubt, apologize profusely.)

Many Mansions would eventually lead me to the Cayce readings on Jesus and the early Christian communities, and everything would begin to fall into place for this formerly very confused Catholic. Thus, the most significant compilation of the Cayce material for me at that time was the book - *Edgar Cayce's story of Jesus*, by Jeffery Furst. From it I learned details of the history of God and Man on Earth, (a portion of it actually <u>before</u> the beginnings of recorded history), and more. Jeffery's biblical acumen, coupled with Edgar's readings, presented a tapestry of characters and events that were both biblically and historically documented.

From the very beginning - *"Let there be Light!"* and the creation of our souls - all the way up to this time, Jeffery's book is as intimately personal in its spiritual depth as it is awe-inspiring in the magnitude of its breadth. Human beings of every time and clime have been joined together in this ongoing evolution-of-consciousness called Life from the very beginning. The Mind and Spirit of the One, trying to reunite with Itself amidst the kaleidoscope of manifested humanity. The One Light, shining through the prisms of each individual "entity". My God, the beauty of us as sparks of that Light, seeking reunion - *with each other!*

<u>We</u> are the countless prisms of the Inner Light that make up the Whole, The Holy One, spoken of throughout time as the living author of every spiritual and religious belief.

Of all the spiritual books I had yet immersed myself in, this was by far the most far-reaching and comprehensive. As poetically written as it is scholarly, it is the most heartfelt effort to explain the true nature of God, the Christ Spirit, and the human soul I have ever been privileged to encounter. It illuminates the actual purpose and meaning of the crucifixion of "self" - what Jesus demonstrated and completed, even unto the actual crucifixion and resurrection of the physical body. Demonstrating for all what it means to be a truly human being – a being of Light, of the nature of its Creator/Source; a Spirit in the flesh, and master over it!

In my not too distant future I would come to know Jeffery, and share a whole summer of sunrise Yoga and afternoon sand-packs. But first, there was another even more auspicious meeting awaiting me.

"Whatever gets you to the Light,

is alright..."

~John Lennon

I began reading every "Cayce book" I could beg, buy, borrow, find in a library, etc.,

[*Mea maxima culpa!,* I even actually stole a copy or two from a local book store - when I met someone who I thought desperately needed what it contained, and I had already given my current copy away and didn't have any money! Jerry Rubin had just published his memoir, *"Steal this Book!"* - setting a fine precedent. But I realized later that I had no right to appropriate anything from anyone who was not a part of our philosophical agreement.]

We *"had all things in common."*, and my friends and I, six of us, shared a stately old multi-level home where we kept all our collective earnings in a large bowl on the kitchen table, and each of us would take whatever we needed for bills, food or clothing, or any personal need that arose. Should I ever encounter the proprietors of the book-store again (and there is <u>no</u> doubt in my mind that I shall) I will be honored to apologize and attempt to balance the scales. The interest alone (on a $3.95 book over 40 years?) must be staggering!

Over time, and coupled with some personal experiments in creative brain-chemistry that were also happening around me at the same time, I found myself firmly on an experiential spiritual path. I was discovering what it truly meant to be a "spiritual seeker", as opposed to merely curious. William James, in 1902, published a book entitled *The Varieties of Religious Experience,* which opened my eyes to the many possibilities of attaining multi-dimensional awareness. I had already read enough about, and experimented with, various consciousness altering disciplines and substances, including, yoga, *prana* breathing, fasting, meditating for hours; as well as mind-altering substances such as marijuana, hashish, and small amounts of Mescaline and LSD.

I recall the very first time I tried "acid", a quarter of a 4-way "hit": after about twenty minutes, I sincerely whispered, "When do we go crazy?" My friend, relieved that at least I wasn't having a "bad" trip, said, "This is it, man." To which I, too, very much relieved, laughingly replied, "Hell, man, I walk around like this!" That was my first hard evidence that I might be just a little more "different" than even I had suspected. Shortly before I finally left for Virginia Beach, however, I had what was a truly defining experience. One that I was most assuredly *not* prepared for.

Early on a Sunday morning, just before dawn, I experienced what can only be called the ultimate "Come to Jesus" moment. Fortunately, I was at that time under a canopy of stars on the very top-floor of a multi-level parking lot in the center of the city, and (very fortunately) looking into the eyes of one of the kindest, purest, most unconditionally loving persons I have ever known.

Just a short while before, I had inadvertently ingested wa-a-ay too much LSD for a relative neophyte like myself. I had been informed that it was "very fresh 4-way Sunshine" – one little tab would do four people nicely.

I was supposed to be attending the small gathering with a date who was unable to make it, but I still had to pay for the two tabs we had committed to. Since I had arrived late for the "trip", and everyone else appeared well on their way (and remembering the somewhat benign effects of my previous experience), I decided I might as well do them both - so I could catch up!

Now, the "expansion" of the mind begins first with the expansion of the ego. First, everything you already believe about your "self" is magnified. While the ego is primarily constructed of past experiences, coupled with hopes and dreams, it is also fraught with doubts and fears - specifically, survival issues. The emotion of fear is so powerful it easily overwhelms the thought processes. When magnified by expanded awareness, and under even imaginary duress, it can create a self-replicating cycle that can be as frightening as it is inescapable. Hence, the tales of those who have "experimented" themselves right into neuroses, sometimes even psychosis.

My only saving grace (and what gave me the *chutzpah* to even attempt such a thing) was my personal conviction that the dark recesses of my mind were just not capable of conjuring up anything even remotely as horrible as what I had already been attempting to live with every day. Indeed, in a futile attempt to save me from myself, my dear cousin Bill - who was at that time the youngest Pa. State Trooper ever to reach the exalted position of *Captain* in the history of the Pennsylvania State Police - gave me what I knew was a sincere and heart-felt warning.

He'd heard that I had been experimenting with hallucinogens and sought me out to say, very strongly, "You had better be careful, brother man. Someday you're liable to see something you can't handle." What I wanted to say, but wouldn't, was, "Like what? Monsters? Demons? What the hell could I possibly see that would be worse than what I have already experienced - in reality!?"

We were looking into each other's eyes as he spoke, and I remember being moved that he cared enough to even do what he was attempting to do. Most of the mutual friends we had grown up with, including our family members, were at a loss to address my situation once outside of the funeral home. They tended to just avoid me, as I said earlier, because I was a brutal, in-your-face, reminder that Life was not at all as safe and predictable as everyone had assumed. Plus, I was by that time a *hippie,* and in our old neighborhood that was not the gentle, harmless, Jesus and Saint Francis emulating, purveyors of God's love we saw ourselves as.

Bill had only meant to help, if he could. What I could not possibly be able to make him understand was - what I already carried within me would dwarf anything Satan himself could dream up, at least for me. Something it didn't appear I was *ever* going to "come down" from. Something that would probably make any actual demons ecstatic, absolutely envious of the pain and confusion it had caused one of God's children. And would continue to cause, for not even God knew how long.

I mean, really: To be personally involved in the decapitation of your beloved newly-wed bride? On the way to your honeymoon?

If I could find him, I would have derisively asked even Satan himself, "So, what have *you* got? Anything? And while you're here, where the hell is God?"

But I could not do that to the guy I knew as "Billy". He was genuinely worried about me. I could only smile warmly at this childhood friend and cousin who was more like a brother. (We had grown up together, and were only a year apart in age. Our mothers were sisters and, for much of our lives, our families shared a "double-block" that had one long front porch and parallel back yards.)

Bill was a year ahead of me in our Catholic "Parochial" School and always academically brilliant, perennial National Honor Society, etc., but I was *way* ahead of him on this one. Absolutely nothing can prepare you for this particular "educational experience", save for the experience itself.

Meanwhile, back on the top level of the Park & Lock, the world I normally inhabited was getting farther and farther away. I was deep in Plato's cave - and it was getting deeper and darker by the moment.

The phrase "cast into outer darkness" floated into my mind, along with other similar thoughts and distorted visions that seemed to be coming from far away. Strange disjointed words in a voice that was sometimes my own, and sometimes unfamiliar leading up to:

"What? Who said that?

"Who said *That?*

"Who's thinking these thoughts?

"Who said *that*?

"Where did *that* thought come from!?

"Me?"

"Who is 'me'?

"Who am 'I'?"

Our bodies were on the roof of a parking garage in the middle of Wilkes-Barre, Pennsylvania. Rising all around us in the pre-dawn darkness were the magnificent Pocono Mountains. Above us, countless stars like you can only see in the thinner drier air of a mountain town.

Even under the roof of that sky, that splendor, I was becoming frightened. In no time at all I seemed to be occupying a couple of different dimensions.

And, for the first time, I felt like I was losing control of my own thoughts. I began to feel fear – I felt I was actually "losing my mind".

With my thoughts, I began to pray. I asked God to protect me. I called Jesus to be with me, over and over, like a mantra.

I turned, slowly, looking for help - and standing there was my dear friend, Andreas.

"Andy" Smith, the strong and pure of heart. And, as always, smiling, filled with joy of life itself - only now, he was also *glowing.* Brightly! He was surrounded by a brilliant white light, as if his body were the wick in a six-foot candle flame. I didn't understand it then, but I was seeing him as his "Christ Self". The part Jesus talks about when He says that we, too, were created in the image and likeness of God, we "...are the Light of the world." The living expressions of that same Light!

I spoke slowly, filled with wonder at his appearance, and half questioningly, "Oh my God, *you're* Jesus?" Andy's smile got even bigger, and he got brighter, and laughing, said, "Wow, man! You're going all the way!" And with that, I perceived a separation between "Andy" and "Michael", and I began to feel as if I was falling backward into myself, careening inward through space.

I looked out at my friends, trying to focus, to stay connected. Off in the distance the sun began coming up, the warm golden light beginning to brighten the sky over the mountaintop.

Suddenly, I felt as if the sun itself was drawing me toward it. As I turned my gaze toward the golden edge of light rising slowly over the top of the mountain, the sun began to shine right <u>through</u> the mountain! I saw that the light was the actual *substance* of the mountain – and the entire physical world! It filled everything with a golden white glow - except for the concrete buildings and streets below us. They seemed dead, like shadows, devoid of life.

Everything else was semi-transparent. I could still see the mountains, but I could also see the Light of which they were made, shining through them and from them! What we refer to so mundanely as "our Sun" was the very Source of Life! The Source of the light and energy that *filled every living thing!* I could see it! The Sun itself was not just Light - it was consciousness! It was <u>Life Itself</u>!

Around and below me the buildings, sidewalks, cars, etc., were darker. They were not "alive". They appeared to be "things", separate from the light, out of context. They were constructed of various sorts of lifeless materials and inserted into this panorama of Living Light! The living things, the mountains, the trees and plants, the air itself – even my friends! – were <u>all</u> made of the Light! It was also all around me in every direction, filling everything I could see with LIFE!

And coming right *through* the mountains was "Our Sun", increasingly brighter toward the center, it now began to appear as a huge circular *Living Diamond*, like a moving kaleidoscopic brilliant white diamond-facetted light! Surrounding the light itself like a living picture frame, were multi-colored clouds of sparkling iridescent pastels that formed the walls of a living tunnel.

Waves of the diamond-facetted, patterns of Light poured outward from the center, rushing toward me, through me, enveloping me, filling 'me' with Light!

It seemed that "I" (not my image, but my presence, my point of reference) was being slowly and gently drawn into this great tunnel of Light, framed all around by the pastel clouds of white, pink, green, blue, violet, with gold lights like stars sparkling inside them, a kaleidoscope of Light flowing into me, and through me.

"I" was being drawn directly into the center, into that enormous diamond of Light that was filling my "self" with peace and warmth, and *Love* such as I had never dreamed of, could never even have imagined, and it was being poured out on all creation. It *was* all creation, in continuous kaleidoscopic waves emanating from the center, enveloping me until I could no longer "observe" it.

I could only surrender to it, "die" to it.

And the more "I" surrendered, the more Light there was! Living Light! Life! Energy of unimaginable power was flowing through me, and absorbing "me" into "IT"

But, "I" was not disappearing - *I was becoming the Light!*

Rising up from within, I began to hear the sound of millions - literally countless millions - of voices all singing in unison. Voices so high, no human ear will ever hear them, voices so low that I felt my body began to vibrate like an earthquake in my physical body, and every note in between.

A voice for every note, in every octave, and every note in between, singing . . .

"A-A-A-A-A-h-h-h-h-h-h-h-h"

Now, I could no longer "see" the light – I could only surrender to it - become the light. My last "thought" was a memory of someone saying: "We are like raindrops falling toward the ocean, fearing our demise. But in that moment when we touch the ocean - we *become* the Ocean." And in the eternal instant, I *became* the Light!

I was, I am, "The ONE"!

The, I AM...

"*I* AM Love . . . *I* AM a sea of Love . . . *I* AM the boundless ocean of Eternal Love. Limitless . . . undying."

I was everywhere, in all things . . . and I <u>was</u> *everyone who ever lived* from the beginning of time. And I saw my Self.

Looking right into "me", from the cross on Calvary. Head hung down, eyes looking up at me, into me. And then "He" winked at "me"! A small hint of a smile! What!?

He was smiling, looking for all the world as if He was trying not to laugh, so as not to spoil the 'drama'!

But, there was no "He", or "me", Only the One. Seeing itself . . . transcendent!

"I" just *was* . . . everything and everyone.

After (literally) an eternity, a light grey mist imperceptibly begins to appear out of nowhere. Ever so slowly, the light slowly disappears into this whitish grey mist. It was as if a veil was simply appearing between "here" and "there", although I still felt that "I" was in both worlds! Even though the light seemed to have disappeared from my sight, "I" was – I am – still part of it!

Just as I was about to form the question, "What was *that*?", in my mind, a voice, in anticipation of my still forming thought, and so loud that I thought everyone there could hear it, spoke:

"The Word!"

My first formed 'thought' was, "Oh, my God!

"In the beginning, was The Word."

"There really is a Word!"

"And there really is a Light!"

Then a memory came floating up all the way from my 1st Grade Catechism: "What is God?": *"God is Love, God is Light."*

Of course! And: *"The Word was made flesh, and dwelt among us."*

That Light? *That* Word? *That* power, the One that created the Universe with a <u>Thought</u>!?

That Light had actually been born into a human body? It's a miracle that the body didn't explode! [*Later in my journey, a Paul Solomon reading would state emphatically: "Know, children, that there is a God so Holy that the human body in its natural state cannot stand his Presence!"*]

Amen, brother!

That Light came into this world without any other identity, any "ego", simply to remind us to *remember!* Jesus prepared and emptied Himself of "self" so that the Light could live in His body - as a human being!

"And this was the true Light, which lighteth everyone that cometh into the world!" [John 1:9] Of

course, deep inside us all, _we_ are that Light! "Ye are *the* light *of the* world." [Mat. 5:14]

I began to weep. What the hell have we been thinking? That light had walked this Earth, in a human body, telling everyone --"I AM The Light!" But, even more importantly: "_You_ are the light of the world!" And, "All that I AM, you are."

I remember an enlightened yogi once described what I had just experienced, as: "The *Dharshan* of the Christ." [*Dharshan* meaning 'visitation'] He added: "Better you should learn to live in the Light, rather than be visited by it." What I *don't* recall is any mention of just how much easier that is to say, than to do.

[Full Stop! Pay attention!]

Right here and now, we must discuss "right here and now", wherever you are: I hope it is obvious to everyone that not every experiment with mind-altering [I actually prefer "consciousness-expanding"] substances will result in my experience.

There is only one way to guarantee that you will have that experience: It is through *fasting*, *mental* (prayer & meditation) and *emotional* (honest awareness of self) disciplines!

Not just dietary changes (although, ingesting less dense food into the body *does* make our bodies less dense - "lighter"), but the sincere calling out of your heart and mind to the "Highest Within" to make Itself known to you; and then, with patience you did not know you were capable of, *"Wait! Wait, I say! Wait upon the Lord."* And in the increasing silence between the thoughts, The Presence begins to be felt, experienced. It is said: "Prepare the container, and it will be filled." We don't need to "do" anything but empty ourselves. Hence, the Buddhist aphorism: "Don't just *do* something, sit there!"

Believe me, "Nature abhors a vacuum". Any mind emptied of preconceptions will be filled with the Light of Life – especially if that is your intention!

The experience I've just described was a gift - the living palpable Grace of God. There was no guarantee I would not get lost in my own imaginings - 'go crazy' - and attempt to fly off the top of that building. I was protected simply because the dominant urge of my heart was to find "God." What I "became" in that moment has been experienced by many, all the "enlightened ones" of <u>every</u> religion. The experiencing of our very souls has been documented in voluminous detail - especially recently through numerous "Near Death Experiences", in our time.

The Light is *real*, far more real than any of our daily concerns and fears, and the Light simply waits within us all, for the moment we stop being who we think we are. There is nothing else separating us from it, and there is nothing we need to do. We need to just cease doing and being those things that actually do make us feel separate from the Light, and from each other:

"Be still, and *know* that I AM God."

The true knowledge and experience of one's own Soul is, in the acquiring of it, not unlike the subtleties and profundities of Shakespeare, or the mind-boggling calculations of Astrophysics. Nothing of either of them is being "hidden" from anyone. Some things must simply be grown into, especially our return to Oneness.

If anything is "hidden", there is ample evidence that it is *we* who are hiding from "It".

The True Journey Begins!

For months following my experience with The Light I wondered what it might mean for me to go to Edgar Cayce's A.R.E. I had no real information about the organization itself, only the books.

I tried to imagine what it might be like to be in the company of people who knew, or at least wanted to know, the same things I sought. And then one day while taking a shower, and shortly after having my copy of *Edgar Cayce's Story of Jesus* disappear from a park bench while I played Frisbee, it came. The voice from beyond my own thoughts clearly said to me: *"Today's the day."*

What?

"Today is the day."

I *knew*, I *saw*, exactly what was being implied.

"But, I've only got 75 cents to my name!"

"Today is the day!"

There were a good number of logical arguments for not going that day, but I had no illusion that any of them was an argument I might win. I knew the voice was right. Everything would be fine. I knew that voice - and the authority of it. I didn't *have* to obey. It was just the right, the only, thing to do.

I had few possessions. Most of us were already sharing everything, or had given away many of the things we once had strived to attain. I had clothing that amounted to a few pairs of jeans and shorts, some shirts and t-shirts, a guitar I was not really committed to but could play. I chose two each of my very favorite t-shirts and shorts, it was late summer and sure to be even warmer where I was headed; a pair of jeans that had been patched and embroidered (by my long-time girlfriend and soul-family-mate, Amber) so many times and so artfully they fit like an artistically decorative second skin. I *loved* them! And I looked so good in them! Oh, yeah! And my bright purple, light corduroy jacket with a "Mr. Natural" patch – high steppin' and wigglin' his finger and saying *"Just passin' through."* above the right breast pocket. I would pack only my very few, very favorite things, (*this is called arranging a major wake-up call!*)

I packed them all, along with a bottle of "Dr. Bronner's" peppermint liquid soap and my toothbrush and toothpaste, etc., all in my also "very special" white canvas over-the-shoulder bag, with the bright golden UFO, hand drawn and colored (by me), with the words *"Swing low, Sweet Chariot"*, around it! Feeling free and easy and in harmony, and leaving behind everything I had been for as long as I could remember - I was off to be *Siddhartha!*

I was taking (almost) nothing with me and had no idea what might happen next. I promised God I would listen closely and do whatever was set before me, and He would make sure I didn't starve or die of exposure. It was in "The Book" and my heart, and I trusted completely.

I walked out the door in the middle of the afternoon and didn't even get off the front steps when my childhood friend George pulled up in his taxi. "Hey, where ya goin, man?"

I started to laugh. I had been wondering how I was going to get all the way across town to the highway leading south to Virginia! George was my mother's favorite amongst my childhood friends because they shared the same birthday. They liked each other a lot and he missed her as much as the family did. Perfect!

I explained to him what I was doing and he *loved* it. He even gave me 5 bucks so I "wouldn't starve until God showed up". That was an inside joke, because we both knew that *he* was being God, in that moment, the first of many aspects of The One (in various states of awakening) that I would be brought together with.

George dropped me off on Rte. 11 South just outside of Wilkes-Barre, and within 5 minutes a car pulled over with two students from a Christian College near Gettysburg, Pa., offering me a ride. God is big on timing.

One of them, the passenger, was apparently handicapped in some way and used crutches or a wheel chair to get around. The crutches stuck up over the front seat beside him and his wheel-chair was in the trunk, and he was not happy about his life-long condition. Over the course of the ride he openly expressed his anger, blaming doctors, drugs that were administered during some complications *in utero,* and anything else that crossed his mind that led to a young lifetime of limitations he felt he did not deserve.

They asked where I was headed and why, and I got my first opportunity to try out my new job, at least as I was beginning to see it. I began to share everything I knew about the different reasons a soul might choose to be hitch-hiking to a place he's never been, or being in a wheel-chair.

Like me during my first awakening to the concept, they were both more than happy to consider that *they* might have had something to do with their current life circumstances, things they had not been consciously aware of.

In order to investigate more fully the possibility of a more specific "why" to the affliction, they insisted I stay over at their dorm so we could talk the night away and maybe make some sense of it all. It would be near dark when we arrived there, so I happily accepted.

We had quite a night, sharing our spiritual understandings in a college dormitory on a very Christian college campus. Also, how 'beliefs' of all kinds continually inform our personal decisions, creating our reality and, ultimately, our experiences. Higher learning, indeed! At their age, many of the things they believed they had absolutely no say in the acquiring or acceptance of. We eventually talked about what Jesus might really have been up to, and how that might play out in all our lives. In the end, a wonderful night.

The following morning, I left the guy in the wheelchair my copy of *Many Mansions,* with the promise that it would change *everything* he thought he knew, and bring him lot closer to Jesus - with a much clearer understanding of what he and Jesus were both "really all about".

Compared to that auspicious beginning, the rest of my journey to Virginia Beach was relatively uneventful – until I finally arrived at the A.R.E., at 67th and Pacific Ave., covered with dried sweat and a fine layer of my own salt. It was a typical "warm" day for a summer in southeastern Virginia (in the low 90's with matching humidity), and I had been standing alongside almost-melting asphalt since Richmond at Interstate 64. All my rides were just a few exits long, and it seemed to take forever between each. By the time I got to the actual oceanfront, plus a ride out to the ARE, the humidity was so dense that the air felt "thick", like I was already underwater! For a guy who lived most of his life in the Pocono mountains, it was an effort just to breathe!

My arrival in what I thought was going to be an earthly part of heaven was, at least weather-wise, beginning to feel an awful lot like, well, hell.

I didn't even bother going up the stairs to what is now called "the old building", a huge grand old 3 story home with a screened in wrap-around veranda, set atop a terraced hill, surrounded by rose gardens in full bloom, with a large dirt and sand parking lot and a clear view of the Atlantic Ocean just across little two-lane Pacific Avenue.

Instead, I turned and walked directly over the dunes to the beach, removing everything I could without getting locked up for exposure, as I walked. There was not a soul in sight except for a handful of people about a mile down the beach, and I was sorely tempted to take off my sweat-soaked shorts and get *au natural*, as well.

I laid down my mystical UFO bag with all my "favorite stuff" in it, putting my sandals and shirt and whatever was in my pockets on top in a pile, and headed the 50 feet or so toward the gently breaking surf.

As a small child, I had been traumatized by an ocean wave that flipped me upside down and threw me back onto the beach at Asbury Park, NJ, scraping my chest on the gravel and pieces of shells on the bottom, and depositing me ignominiously in a half-drowned heap, like an insignificant piece of flotsam just a few feet in front of the rest of my family. Over their laughter, and my tears, I swore never to go near it again - and I never did! But now, I eagerly walked, staggering through the hot ankle-deep sand, into the cool welcoming waves until the water was up to my neck - and took off my shorts.

The ocean water was cool, compared to the air, and *alive* and moving. I could feel it caressing my skin, causing me to sway gently in its undulations, welcoming me like a living thing. I almost laughed with relief - and joy. I felt, actually *knew,* I was being baptized - released from yesterdays. I could feel myself becoming "a new creature". I belonged to Life now! And Life was this gentle but enormously powerful force moving me effortlessly. It was rocking me, this cradle of Life, apparently trying to show me (and anyone else) a good time. It was that clear, obvious. Some would say I was being embraced by The Mother, the living Spirit of the Earth, the source of our bodies; that my Soul was reuniting with its Source, the Creative Forces, the Ocean of love that is the Universe in which everything exists. . .

. . . and they would be absolutely correct.

I was in "eternity" - where the past had passed, and the present was unfolding moment by moment. I began dipping beneath the waves, into the silence, staying completely under for a minute or two at a time, over and over, merging with the ocean. I actually had to resist the urge to "breathe" the water - I felt so naturally a part of it. The ocean surrounding me was the same water I was made of! My body *was* of the ocean, literally.

Later, I would learn about the human *aura* - the electro-magnetic field that we actually are. How that energy that is us, as Souls, joins with the life-force that is the ocean, and merges our consciousness with the Source of Life itself anytime we enter into the oceans of the world. I felt renewed, profoundly peaceful - and finally ready to meet the people who had created those books.

As I walked out of the ocean (with my shorts back on), I went to the spot where I left my things. I had placed them right where I had walked into the water, a straight line between the end of the path through the dunes and the water's edge, but they were nowhere to be seen. I walked back and forth to the path in the dunes, up and down the beach – gone!

There had not been a soul in sight, except for the few people far down the beach when I first arrived, but they were gone too.

This was crazy! The bag, my shirt, socks and sneakers, could not have just disappeared, could they? After looking in the only 55 gallon green-barrel garbage can in sight, and searching all the way up into the dunes, I eventually had to admit that they had just disappeared. Never mind that this was not possible - everything I had was gone except for the shorts on my behind.

Now I really did feel like Siddhartha - and I was 500 miles from anyone I had ever known.

I *loved* that bag! And I really loved the things in it. My favorite pieces of clothing, and my personal hygiene articles, plus the sneakers, socks, and the shirt I had been wearing. In my attempt to leave my "self" behind and become new, *I only brought the things that meant the most to "me"*. A more ridiculous gesture of divestiture could hardly be imagined.

I was really asking for it – and I got *exactly* what I was asking for.

I had no choice but to walk across the street to the ARE, in nothing but a pair of wet shorts and hope for the best.

Across the little two-lane-street, through the dirt parking lot, and up the long concrete stairways that bisected the terraced Rose gardens, to where a beautiful inlaid stone centerpiece filled the center of the great stone plateau of a courtyard. Two gracefully curving stairways lead from there up to the porch and the entrance to the library and offices. Slowly, I walked into the exact center of the *mandala*-like stone formation and stood there in silence, at first just thinking I might give my shorts a little time to dry off. Instead I was overwhelmed by a sense of the ending of a journey. That spot was the physical expression of the 'center' I had been unconsciously seeking. I felt I had finally arrived at a destination I had long been travelling toward.

There is a labyrinth there now, the center of it in the exact same spot signifying the same awareness. I guess I was just a few decades early.

Throughout my decades of involvement with the ARE I have consistently found that almost every one of the literally millions of visitors who have arrived here are first touched with a sense of "coming home". Not a physical home, but the soul quickening with the knowing that, here, _it_ is at home - for here, the soul is the focus, even when the research is for purely physical healing or any other information. The Soul recognizes that it has entered a truly spiritual place. A place where neither religion nor scientific discipline need be left behind, merely integrated. God lives, and makes sense, He or She just has a different agenda from the ego – and that should not be news to anyone.

Standing in that open space, the ocean behind me and the Library before me, absent anything of the physical world but my shorts, I was truly empty. I remember thinking, _Siddhartha_ indeed! I didn't even have a bowl! Thank God there was a box of flip-flops to slip on just outside the front door, for random beachgoers who might wander in out of curiosity. After a quick prayer for mercy (and guidance I might be able to recognize) in I wandered.

It was called "the lobby" but it was more like walking into someone's living room, except for the small desk just ahead and off to the right, behind which sat a slight serene mature woman with perfectly coiffed hair, attired impeccably in a simple blue skirt and white blouse, (with no doubt 'sensible' shoes under the desk).

There were a number of stuffed chairs in floral-print covers with table lamps alongside, a few framed pictures on the walls, some live plants here and there throughout, and the kind of serene but well lived-in quiet one might associate perhaps with your grand-mother's home.

There at the left end of the lobby was an open doorway leading to a tiny room called "the book store". Opposite it on the other side of the room was a doorway that opened on a flight of stairs that led to the second floor offices. Immediately to the right, when you entered the front door, were French-doors opening into "the library". It was all just as clean and tidy as your grandma's house, including the library.

I, on the other hand, looked like an uncertain almost naked version of Jesus, with a touch of drowned rat. Smiling warmly (and without a bit of sarcasm or irony) the dignified woman behind the desk said absolutely sincerely, "How *very* nice to see you. Is this your first time visiting with us?"

Attempting to be equally sincere, I replied, "Why, thank you. Yes, it is. And I promise you, I had an entirely different appearance when I began my journey to your establishment." Still smiling warmly, she asked, "Is there anything specific that you were wanting to find?" And I, as graciously as possible because I was still absolutely sincere, replied, "Well, yes. Maybe a T-shirt. And perhaps a job so that I might replace my clothing, and everything else that was just taken from me on the beach across the street."

She asked me to explain, and I began to relate as well as I could how I came to be standing before her with nothing on but damp shorts and a pair of their flip-flops. She listened intently and was about to say something when someone sitting and reading in one of the chairs smilingly offered me a white t-shirt from their back-pack. Perfect! And, it fit.

The receptionist, I would later learn, was named Ann Clapp, and she gently asked me to wait there while she went to see if the Director of the A.R.E. had time to see about an emergency job. He asked to meet me in person!

I crossed the room and entered the doorway that led to the stairs to the second floor. As I turned to walk up them, I instantly beheld a fairly large painting of Jesus on the wall facing me, at the top of the stairs. He is standing with welcoming open arms surrounded by a light aura of white, and His eyes looked right into mine.

He appeared almost physically real - the feeling was definitely real.

Walking softly up the flight of stairs, while looking into those eyes, was a profound experience. I felt as if I was literally walking up a stairway into a higher state, specifically to meet with the Christ. It was almost a relief to reach the top landing and stop for a moment, assimilating the energy. I would not have been able to talk, or make sense, if I hadn't.

I turned left at the top of the stairs, as I had been instructed, to the office of Dr. Herb Puryear, Director. He was seated behind a large desk, impeccably attired in what I could assume was a fairly expensive suit.

Dr. Puryear was somewhat older than I, but still quite young. Warm, friendly, and very business-like, he immediately asked for the details of my experience. Very sincere in his concern (I discovered later that he was an M.D. and a Psychiatrist) he explained that there really were no jobs available, but I would be welcome to stay in the building referred to as "210", across the street alongside the ARE, and to take part in the Work/Study program. That would allow me to partake of some conferences and other programs in exchange for work that needed to be done around the grounds. In much of the world, this is also known as *Karma Yoga*.

After a short conversation about the decisions and experiences that had brought me to be in front of him at that moment, which he pursued with a trained psychiatrist's eye and ear, and the soul of a mystic (he was the Director of the A.R.E., for God's sake!), he added, "Whether you take part in that or not, though, you definitely need some clothing." Then he reached for his wallet and took out a fifty-dollar bill, offering it to me with the words: "You can pay me back when you get settled. From all you just told me, you are where you're supposed to be. I have no doubt you will be successful at whatever you do."

He stood and shook my hand, and said with a genuinely warm smile, "Good luck. I'm sure we'll be seeing each other again."

I left Dr. Puryear and hitch-hiked into town. I was pleased to be informed by my ride that I was in "T-Shirt Town", so named because of the plethora of stores whose primary purpose was to sell T-shirts and such, all decorated with various pithy sayings about the joys of being in Virginia Beach. It took a little while before I found someone who would sell me a half dozen of his shirts blank, for a reasonable price.

The beach-front was completely tourist oriented. There was one Rose's store and no real Super-Market, so any actual "shopping", for groceries, clothing, etc., would have to be done in a "shopping center" quite a bit away from the beach proper. I was able to find a couple pairs of jean-shorts and some white long-pants, as well as some sandals and a belt. With still a few dollars left for food, things were definitely looking better.

The Monastery is Open!

When I went back out to the A.R.E., I was feeling a little more secure. There was free coffee in the book store area, and always at least a few like-minded people. They were from all parts of our country and the world, and they too were searching, or researching, for things they could not access elsewhere - anything from physical healing to spiritual enlightenment, usually both.

Just in the course of having spontaneous conversations with whoever was about, I was gifted with a very light summer-weight sleeping bag and the information that, while it was actually illegal to sleep on the beach, that ordinance was aimed more at revelers passing-out in the sand fifty blocks south, down at the 'tourist' end of the beach. One could be just unobtrusive enough, this far away from "town", to find a secluded spot in the dunes for a decent night's rest. As rustic as that might sound, it turned out to be the most civilizing and life-changing interlude in my life, bar none.

That first night in town, after the ARE closed at 10 PM, I went across to the beach and while walking the narrow wooden pathway that led through the dunes, discovered that there was a little "hollow" on the top that could not be seen directly from the water level. Perfect! I would be invisible to any passers-by, even the police patrolling the beach. Once when I was sitting on top of the dune meditating, a policeman on a small motorcycle shined a light my way, and I had no choice but to wave in a friendly manner. That seemed to satisfy him. He waved back and continued alongside the water and off into the night.

It is virtually impossible to accurately convey what happens to you when you are lying on your back on a beach in the dark of a warm summer's night - which gives you virtually a 360 degree panorama of a star filled sky that is essentially, uncountable diamonds sparkling on black velvet.

The almost complete absence, of what we have come to call "ambient light" - such as street lights, tall buildings, homes, all the things we've come to just accept as the way it is in our "civilized" world - creates an entirely different experience for the mind.

Going to sleep under the stars, away from town by a couple of miles, nestled in the hollow of the sand dunes just off the water, and with the sound of the surf like God's own subliminal program - you are going far away, guaranteed. And when you fall asleep to that, after bathing your eyes and soul in the great cosmic vista of the Universe laid out before you for as long as you can keep your eyes open, along with the real "Mother Ocean" providing a never-ending soundtrack? Well, you just haven't got a chance of staying crazy.

The sound of those waves playing seamlessly throughout the night will lift you to the spiritual realms, stimulating dreams of the highest nature. Coming back to this world with the soft brightening of the morning sky, like the birds and other animals, means you don't actually "wake up". No. You very gently, imperceptibly, become aware that you are *aware*. The sound of the waves is not a 'new' or obtrusive sound. It's the seamless soft *whoosh* of the waves onto the sand, then a moment of silence, then another wave, that you have already been "listening to" all night. It is more like a soft audible pulse bringing you back to awareness of your body. It is also a part of your soul, gently awakening the hearing part of your brain, changing only your point of reference – not the experience.

You have been hearing that sound, uninterrupted all night. It is in you. It is a part of you. It is the song of what the Source called, the *You* of you. Any parts of you that were "separated" from any other have been seamlessly reintegrated by the sound of the ocean waves constantly meeting the sand, because you know that *that* sound has been going on forever. And *that* sound, and the memory of it in your soul now reestablished, will be with you for the rest of this life, and beyond. Should you do this for a number of days (I did it for most of a summer, well into autumn!) you will be changed. Your ability to live in *alpha-state* will be so natural a part of your being that you will have to make a conscious effort to get "lost in thought" again. It will permanently change your way of being in the world. You will be re-harmonized with Life.

The Ocean itself, as we experience it, is first and foremost an "idea" of God that exists on all levels of creation. What we call the physical or "natural" world, especially the ocean, *is* the living Spirit of the Creative Forces in material form. The sound of it will make us one with it - because that is who and what we naturally are. Between swimming in it daily, and sleeping next to it, "I" had been taken into the primal waters on all levels, washed clean, polished up bright and shiny, and (gently, this time) returned to the world.

Welcome to the 'real' world, my soul. Let the transformation begin!

To that end, I began the disciplines necessary to transcend my normal thought processes and learn to listen with, and to, my heart: keeping a dream journal; eating very lightly; meditating all times of day and night; morning Yoga and "sand-packs" on the beach - with *Jeffery Furst,* the aforementioned author of *Edgar Cayce's Story of Jesus!* - and absorbing myself in the collected and collated readings - as well as the many collections and books focusing on specific subjects such as Diet & Health, Music, Healing – literally, *ad infinitum.*

It has been said that the ARE Library is itself the reincarnation of the Great Library of Alexandria, Egypt, which was at that time the repository of the world's wisdom teachings from the beginning of recorded knowledge, destroyed thousands of years ago by superstitious barbarians. I found that not just the knowledge, but the very Gnosis of the Living God, was here to be experienced in whatever discipline one was trained in; whether arts and music, medicine, psychology, religion, philosophy, mathematics, celestial sciences, etc., all the paths to understanding the nature and grandeur of Life itself.

And all paths lead to that One Great Truth:
The oneness of all Life – with the possibility, and
God's hope, for all humanity to come to conscious
realization of that state of connectedness through
self-mastery. Life's only purpose is for all human
beings to come to know themselves to be themselves,
yet still one with God.

While absorbing all this in the ARE Library, I
made the acquaintance of a retired Air Force
noncom, one Donald Button, whose personal
discipline was Astrology. Imagine that. He looked like
a slightly heavier version of an old 1950's TV
character, "Wally Peepers". He did my birth-chart for
me and taught me how to research the meaning of
the different "aspects": Trines, Squares, Oppositions,
Conjunctions, etc. To assist me in gaining actual
"self knowledge", he directed me to an extensive and
comprehensive series of books explaining <u>every
degree of every aspect of each planet *and* its
influence upon the mind and Soul</u>. Donald taught me
how to read and understand these things, and,
needless to say, I was a very willing student.
Astounding! And astoundingly accurate as an
explanation of the inner urges and predilections we
all live our lives responding to. Creation was a living
thing! And we are moving around in the midst of it
all, creating with our thoughts, our fears and our
desires, the events and circumstances we experience
as our lives! Our free will, with which we decide how
to respond to the urging of our minds our bodies and
our Souls, is always the determining factor, of
course, and it is vital to know that we can and do
control every decision of our lives. It is also nice to be

aware of, and truly understand, the source of our inner impulses and feelings - and thus *not* be a slave to them.

One day, as I was searching through the many Ephemeris' and accompanying texts for the understanding of the various aspects, I found Don chuckling over a chart. I whispered that, "I didn't know these things could be amusing." And he replied, "It's yours! I'm just enjoying the confluence of certain influences for the years ahead and all I can say is: whatever you do, make sure you're right, because everybody will be watching." Many years later, all I can say is, he was right. All of this which I had been accepting as the *culmination* of my search, the completion, was actually just the beginning of my real education - the preparation process for my *Dharma*, my reason for being on Earth at this time. Until then, no matter how insane it felt or appeared, my Life had been only a "prep" school. Now, it was time for the "Universe-University!"

The Association for Research and Enlightenment, and The Edgar Cayce Foundation, are well known in both the United States and abroad. Edgar Cayce "Centers" exist in 37 countries, and there are active members in more than 70 nations around the world. The A.R.E. community is a global network.

Thanks to the printing and communication breakthroughs of our time, Brother Edgar has become one of the most famous "psychics" in history. But, to see him as merely a "psychic" is to completely miss the true nature of the gift he and others like him (and, yes, there have been others like him throughout history) have brought to humanity.

From before the beginning of recorded history there have been "prophets." In the Judeo-Christian tradition they provided the text for what most of us know as The Bible, both of the "Old Testament" and much of the "New". Around the world, they have continuously contributed translations of divinely inspired Wisdom to humankind as the needs and the self-knowledge of humanity evolved.

Today, our exponentially increasing awareness of the nature of our world and the Universe in which we live, demands continuous updating, from our own planet and Solar system and the enormity of our own galaxy, beyond to other Galaxies - distances so vast that they must be measured in light years - all the way back down the scale to cellular, molecular, even sub-atomic reality, and the "bio-electric" nature of our own bodies and minds!

Obviously, all of this would be ill-served by simply more "dogma".

Understanding is *demanded* of us. Real understanding! <u>Experiential</u> knowledge, not just belief - is the key to the door of Reality. True Self-knowledge, the conscious awareness of one's own inextricable connection with Life, *and* each other - that is the true Holy Grail!

Unfortunately, when we hear the word "prophet" we tend to imagine bearded men in animal skins or sack-cloth, living in some wilderness, coming into civilization to deliver great portents of doom. But the word "prophet" is most commonly defined as simply, "Someone who interprets Divine Will". That simple phrase says an awful lot, and anyone who could actually _do_ that would be enthusiastically welcomed by everyone, you would think. Well, not usually. More precisely, not usually until after they are dead.

Jesus himself (and we all know what happened to Him!) was considered by almost everyone in his time to be a prophet. Until His resurrection only one or two of his closest disciples dared even consider He might be more; certainly Mohammed, the founder of Islam, is still referred to by his disciples as "The Prophet"; here in America we had Joseph Smith, finder of the Golden Tablets and founder of the Mormon faith; Edgar Cayce has long been known far and wide as "The Sleeping Prophet" - God is demonstrably ecumenical. [_The word "ecumenical", by the way, means: "Involving or promoting friendly relations between different religions."_ Now that sounds like a God we can all get behind.] And let us not forget the famous, at least in our time, Michel de Nostradamus. Hardly known in his own time, he gained great respect and recognition, albeit posthumously, from the interpretation and mass publishing of his _Quatrains_ (and more than a few television specials) in ours.

Prophets are those who, by altering their consciousness - releasing the world's hold on their minds through fasting, prayer and meditation, deprivation of the senses, etc., invite union with the highest within themselves - the Divine Mind, or Source mind, if you will - and are thus able to bring into our world the wisdom and understanding that serves to inspire and assist in human enlightenment, and life lived in harmony with Divine purpose.

Indeed, the first half of the Judeo-Christian Bible is composed almost entirely of a series of "prophetic" discourses that helped guide the Hebrew people, and even predicted the entrance of the Christ Spirit, the *Solar Logos*, "The Word" into human form. It concludes with John's apocalyptic prophecy, *The Book of the Revelation*, which describes a cataclysmic end to the physical world and the decimation of humankind by earthquakes, floods and pestilence.

The "spiritual" interpretation of John's *Revelation* - as given through the Cayce material in a comprehensive study done over several years - describes the seven "churches" and "candlesticks" as the seven glands and centers of the endocrine system that also coincide with eastern spiritual teachings of the "chakras". These are described as bio-energy vortexes whereby the Soul connects with the physical body. The earthquakes and upheavals, *et al*, occur in consciousness as the ego/personality battles for survival while the Soul seeks reunion with its Creator.

That makes that famous book of prophecy, by far, the most well-known and least-understood prophetic offering ever! Very few recognize it in the true way, but those who do are well on their way to the real Holy Grail of fully realized Self.

These "divine interventions" into whatever is passing for civilization at the time, very often evolve into belief systems. Systems which, when adhered to, *should* promote health and harmony in those who adopt them, and often led to the birth of many of the world's religions and philosophical disciplines.

It is important to note that the guidelines put forth in these systems usually began as simple innocent attempts to guide human behavior in a positive way, often ameliorating the inability to comprehend certain things (like the complex functioning of the digestive system) with, "God said", all simply to inspire the local humans to more positive health paradigms, spiritual growth, or societal change. This often entailed the warning that ignoring the well-meant suggestion could lead to everything from personal suffering to cultural collapse, even global disaster! Be that as it may, most of those ancient guidelines stemmed from what we *now* consider common sense, thanks to our increased knowledge and more sophisticated understanding of that which was just not understandable in earlier times.

Perhaps the best example of this is the *Kosher* discipline of not ingesting meat and dairy at the same meal, as given to the ancient Hebrews, the earliest blessed recipients of imminently practical Real Life guidance.

It began as a warning based on a scientifically sound fact: Milk will curdle in the high heat of the stomach, quickly forming a yogurt like mass that prevents digestive juices and acids from reaching and dissolving the meat. Thus the meat, still in the 100+ degree (F) heat of the stomach and intestines, will putrefy and literally poison the person.

It is amazing, and more than a little amusing (at least to this affectionate *goyem*), to see how that simple common sense suggestion to keep those two food types <u>separate within the stomach and digestive system</u> evolved over five-thousand years into two entire collections of kitchen tools and utensils Indeed, dual sets of anything and everything that either food group would *ever* touch - either in the preparation or the consumption thereof - i.e., two complete sets of dishes, bowls, cups, silverware, pots, pans, knives, forks, spoons, *everything*!

This is what my observant, or *Kosher,* friends deal with every day. Forgive me if it seems that the greatest actual beneficiaries of such severe discipline appear to be the manufacturers of the kitchenware! One can only hope many lives have been saved.

Two things make Edgar Cayce's work unique: First, was the admonition from the Source to make absolutely certain that the wisdom that came through Edgar would <u>never</u> become a pseudo-religion, or any other form of "schism or ism". It was always about the information itself - the knowledge and guidance designed to awaken divine-awareness within anyone, and everyone - reuniting all mankind in the oneness of God, the Love, from which we all came forth.

Second, was the particular time in which Cayce was born - the dawn of mass communication! For the first time in recorded history the entire world was becoming "connected". Edgar's first reading occurred in the year 1901. That was also the moment of the birth of radio and the beginning of mass publishing. Newspapers and magazines would follow soon thereafter and be sold on street corners, and shortly after that - delivered right to our homes!

He would be the first prophet of God to have his effort disseminated, not just by "oral tradition", animal skins or parchment, but on the pages of books - which could be published in the many thousands – and newspapers, everyday by the millions! Still later, there would be radio and television news, with reporters broadcasting from around the world, and numerous "specials" created for global networks such as The Discovery Channel, the A&E Network, The Learning Channel, etc.

Still, the message brought through Cayce was the same as that in all monotheistic religions and spiritual disciplines from the beginning of time: "God is One", and *we* are the living expression of that Life Force! We are The One, comically (were it not for all the suffering caused) believing we are all separate individuals, and our different appearances (like skin color) only magnify those differences and negate our similarities, even our universal blood-types. In our Souls, though, it is quite a different matter.

As one Cayce reading explained the ancient verse, "Know ye, O Israel, the Lord thy God is One": *"Yea, though there be other systems, galaxies, even universes, the Soul of man - thine own Soul! – encompasses all of these!"* There is nowhere to hide from that eternal Truth . . . except in our own minds.

Cayce's readings also describe Atlantis, where the Children of the Law of One fought against the

Sons of Belial - "the lie" of separation. This is significant because our time is a replaying of those same conflicts by those same Souls, complete with the rediscovering of the same "forces" and power that destroyed their world in that time. (More on that, later.) They also contain dietary guidelines for today that mirror those established by most religions. The nutritional recommendations for healing diseases and other problems are always centered on returning the body to its natural state. The foundation of this is that our bodies are reflections of the Earth itself, and the imbalances in our systems that create all of our health problems are always due to ingesting too much, or not enough, of the elements of which our bodies and the Earth are made. The lack or overabundance of any of the vitamins, minerals and trace elements creates imbalance and causes "disease". Exacerbating all this is that much of what we ingest today is completely foreign to our bodies, "processed" foods many of us have been fed virtually from birth.

Restoring the body's balance would cure the physical problems, but they were just as often the product of an imbalance in the mental or emotional state. It is no secret today that out thoughts and emotions have a profound effect on our bio-chemistry. Prayer, combined with meditation (talking to God, *and* listening within to the Divine for guidance) was always the best "medicine". The true goal of every soul is the returning of one's physical life back into harmony with Spirit; Consciousness of the creator in us, and everywhere in the Infinite Universe. Mentally, emotionally and spiritually, the triune harmony of a truly "human" being, would best be accomplished by learning to see "self" in others, friend and foe. Because of our inherent oneness, our lives are always a mirror of our thoughts and feelings - and "mind is the builder!"

Obviously, the information coming through Cayce transcended the barriers of time and space. The "readings" speak of the creation of our souls "in the beginning" and describe not just the actual history of that which informs our scriptures, but the aforementioned prior civilizations such as Atlantis and Mu. Even the other planets of our solar system are experiences for our souls between earthly lives. In, or on, these "other spheres" we simply inhabit higher vibratory dimensions not perceivable by the narrow spectrum allowed by the human eye. These are levels of light and energy that we already acknowledge and even use daily, such as: Infra-red, ultra-violet, X-Ray, etc., "invisible" to the human eye, but most assuredly and demonstrably real.

While the oft repeated phrases such as "God is not mocked!"; "Whatsoever a man sows, that must he also reap"; were all reassuring, as they illuminated an inescapable but purposeful justice that would be reconciled over vast amounts of what we call time, they also caused my heart to ache with the question, "My God! What could I possibly have done to cause this to happen to us, to that beautiful and innocent child who had been my bride, my life?"

The answer to that would be a long time coming, fortunately, because such truths, by the grace of God, absolutely *must* be grown into.

Of all the people from all the places around the world that I met at the ARE, one man - because we both understood vibration, specifically music, as the actual nature of the Divine - had a uniquely significant and profound effect on my life. Beginning with the education he gave me about the ability of music to heal and transform lives - from attitudes and emotions, to tissues and even organs - but also because of a situation he helped create, albeit unknowingly, that would change so many lives, and continues to do so.

His name is Joel Andrews and he was a world-class classically trained harpist, acknowledged as one of the founders of the "New Age" music genre, beginning back in the late sixties and early seventies.

Joel also appeared with luminaries of Jazz and New Age, including the Paul Winter Consort, and was acknowledged as having discovered a number of "new" sounds on the harp – an instrument already thousands of years old! - not the least of which, to me, was "slide" harp: using the tuning wrench to slide up and down the different strings, just like a slide guitar, but with a much more ethereal and hypnotic sound. Loved it!

Like me, he had come to Virginia Beach to study at the ARE, where music was described in the Cayce readings as "...the bridge between the worlds of Spirit and matter." As we know today, all matter, even the cells of our bodies, are made up of atoms and molecules vibrating at different rates. One can re-harmonize a bodily organ, such as a liver or a heart, by playing the proper notes and corresponding chords with "intention". This physically creates a sympathetic vibration, just as a "high-E" string will sympathetically vibrate on a six-string guitar when the "low-E" string is stuck, and *vice versa*. The sound vibration of the proper note or chord could promote the actual physical healing of the 'dis-eased' organ because those sound waves have distinct physical properties. And, if the creator of the sound was consciously trying to facilitate a healing, mental, physical or emotional, that desire would also be transmitted, both in Spirit/Mind and on the physical sound waves themselves to the ailing body, and would stimulate and inspire healing. That's why we all listen to music, of any kind. We acknowledge the profound effect it has on us on many levels.

Joel would have people come by the beautiful home that five of us were sharing which had a large "great room", big enough for his harp and assembled percussion instruments with plenty of space left over. People would arrive and lie on a mat on the floor near the harp, and Joel would "channel", or intuit, a unique piece for each soul that would also be taped and given to that person for further applications and use afterwards. Truly miraculous healings and other extraordinary occurrences were not uncommon.

We often played as a quartet known as *The Order of Orpheus,* when we played at various functions - anywhere and everywhere, from churches and spiritual organizations to local hospitals, even prisons, etc. Which is how we found ourselves doing:

"The Gig that Changed Everything!"

Next: *"They Meet!"*

They Meet!

We were to precede a lecture to be given by The Reverend Paul Solomon, be the "opening act", so to speak. "We" were *The Order of Orpheus*: Joel Andrews, world-class, classically-trained and internationally acclaimed harpist, mystic, and healer; Michael Rybak on Flute; Pat Gomol, vocals; and I on percussion.

My percussion ensemble consisted of an array of hand drums: a Djembe, Bongos, an African 'Talking' Drum, a pair of Indian Tablas; as well as an assortment of tambourines, shakers, rattles, cymbals of all kinds, and an 18" Tibetan Gong. Rounding it all out was an array of *instruments-in-name-only* that would have made the original "Spike Jones" proud. These were 'found' items that Joel had simply happened upon, all of which produced unique and (in the right context) oddly beautiful sounds. They included such nonmusical items as steel brake drums, 1 each from 13", 14" and 15" automobile wheel assemblies; a 1970's era *Oldsmobile F-85* hubcap that just happened to be a perfect C-Major gong; a stainless-steel restaurant quality in-sink dish-drainer, etc.

As any percussionist can verify, if an object can make a sound and you "play" it at precisely the proper moment, *presto,* that sound becomes music and the object is, at least for that moment, a musical instrument. The key phrase here is: "the proper moment." As I once informed my musical prodigy son early in his life: "If you make exactly the right sound at precisely the right moment, people will applaud and give you money. If you make that exact same sound at the wrong time, they will make you go to bed." In life, timing is everything - as we shall see.

Our job was to create a "sacred space", a spiritual-meditative atmosphere for Paul Solomon and those who had come to hear him. In his own words, Paul was "a fourth-generation Southern Baptist Minister from the buckle of the Bible Belt!" A devout man, whose great-grandfather was one of the old "circuit-rider" preachers during the expansion of the West. Paul described him as "a preacher with a Bible in one hand, Colt Peacemaker in the other, for snakes . . . of all kinds."

The Reverend William Dove, Paul's actual birth name, had inadvertently and somewhat traumatically acquired the same "psychic" ability as Edgar Cayce, described as a "full-trance channel". That is, the individual Soul leaves the body, and there is virtually zero (*Delta* to *Theta* level) brain-wave activity, even while "...*reading from these records...*" Needless to say your everyday Southern Baptists wanted nothing to do with that, and so the good Reverend Dove was on his own. Good for us!

His "reading" in this state had been verified during EEG sessions at the J.B. Rhine Institute for Parapsychological Studies at Duke University in 1972, and I could hardly wait to hear him speak. Most of us in Virginia Beach, as well as the untold thousands throughout the world already familiar with the Cayce material, had long lamented that Edgar seemed to be the only human who had that particular gift. I would find out during my coming work with Paul that he was merely the last in a long line of such prophets, and, as mentioned earlier, Edgar was merely the first of that long line to benefit from relatively recent breakthroughs in mass communication.

It was said Paul was going to speak that day about the nature of God as Consciousness, as well as The Great Pyramid, UFO's, meditation, and personal spiritual awakening. In other words, he was going to cover in one talk all of my own life-long personal research subjects! Research that began back in high-school where I had been labeled a "chronic truant", because I spent a couple of days a week in the enormously enlightening Osterhout Free Public Library in Wilkes-Barre, Pa., just a short walk across the center of downtown from James M. Coughlin High School (studiously avoiding the brain-numbing boredom of ingesting and repeating facts in the name of education). This was during the late 1950's, and Parapsychology, Psychic Research, etc., already had their own Dewey Decimal section, 133, as I recall. A more delicious and satisfying intellectual diet for a curious teenager could hardly be found!

It is interesting to note that the Library itself had once been a very large Cathedral like church, with high vaulted ceilings supported by marble columns. Inside, the sun shone through large stained glass windows, while long cylindrical chandeliers hung on even longer chains from the ceiling. And then there was the quiet. A deep warm and welcoming stillness one only finds in places where a hundred years of prayer and meditation have charged the very walls and every object.

With that early preparation, and the ensuing years spent perusing the Cayce material and religious mystics and saints of every faith and no faith, I was well prepared for the good Rev. Solomon's presentation. Plus, I was in the band! Always a great way to get to meet the "headliner".

Little did I know!

The "stage", at the east wall of the *Aquarian Age Yoga Center* (formerly the altar, when it was a Christian church) was large enough to provide plenty of room for our small group. Joel's symphony size harp, an instrument that looks pretty much like the insides of a Grand Piano turned upside-down and sideways, was in the center. Patricia and Michael were on one side and I was on the other, with my myriad percussion instruments placed all around me . . . and a guy who would inadvertently change a lot of lives forever, sat just a foot or two to my left.

John David was a long time friend of Joel. He was a psychology professor at a university in Florida and visiting Joel while on sabbatical. Joel asked me if I would mind if John David accompanied us on stage that day, just to "add a little percussion". I figured it was essentially Joel's group, and he obviously knew him well, so if he thought it was OK, it surely was with me.

John David shared that long-haired, high-forehead, wide-eyed, big-grin, happily intense, somewhat crazed, demeanor that Mick Fleetwood has when he is in the groove of an up-tempo *Fleetwood Mac* tune. Except, John David had that look all the time! I recall Joel mentioning that John David's academic orientation was the Fritz Perls school of Gestalt Therapy. Though I was unfamiliar with it at the time, I discovered much later that that particular modality of *Gestalt* is based on Perls' book: *Ego, Hunger and Aggression.* That little bit of information would explain a great deal of what was about to happen, though it still could not have prepared me for it. Of course, the organizing of disparate sounds (and people) into a harmonious whole is the very nature of music – so let the games begin!

There we were in this quiet and holy place, designed specifically to leave the outer world behind for the higher realms within. Having already been a church of one kind or another for four or five decades, it was unquestionably a place of spiritual purpose.

We were to play for fifteen or twenty minutes. Our first piece was more a harmonizing of the group with the audience, establishing that subtle but powerful communication necessary between musicians and those listening. The second piece, though, was truly transcendent, and finished in a gentle hypnotic *decrescendo,* embodying the journey from the outer world of the senses to a receptive silence within.

It brought the audience and our little group into perfect stillness, the last notes sparkling from the highest end of the chimes and fading into the deep silence. We were all there together, eyes closed, minds and hearts open, completely attuned to the moment.

John David ("Bless his heart", as they say about such folks here in the South), apparently felt that moment needed a little more closure. Unseen and completely unexpected by anyone else in the building (who were all experiencing together the desired "Prime Central Stillness"), John David picked up the rock-hard percussion mallet I normally used to gently play those steel brake drums, and gave what's called in the music business, a *fortissimo strike* - or, "good solid whack" - to that 18 inch Tibetan Gong, which I had positioned directly alongside of me.

In that deep profound and perfect silence, the explosion of sound so near to my body hit me like a punch in the stomach!

I almost keeled right over. My whole body felt as if it were vibrating cartoon-like along with the gong, which was now swinging insanely back and forth, creating never before heard waves of overtones throughout the room. I literally became physically nauseous and thought I was going to throw up right onstage. I looked at John David with the same wild-eyed look he usually had - minus the grin.

I half fell over, and began to crawl off the stage to my right, on my hands and knees, fighting the nausea, past Joel, then Pat, and Michael – and headfirst into the shins of Paul Solomon. I looked up, He was cradling a good size Bible in the crook of his right arm, standing very erect, looking back down at me, and smiling. I tried to smile back, but could manage only a weak grin. I didn't even feel connected to my face. I was dizzy and it was all I could do to keep my balance even on my hands and knees.

I almost fell down the small single step that led off the altar. Behind me, Paul had stopped, slowly turning his head. Our eyes met again as he watched me quizzically over his shoulder, while I attempted to negotiate that last stair. I eventually made it to my feet and headed for the door as quickly as I could, in real fear of throwing up on the pristine cream-colored Yoga Center carpeting. I sat on the outside steps for a few minutes until I was able to walk.

The applause when Paul was introduced wafted out of the windows as I began walking the three or four blocks toward the beach, eventually collapsing in the sand and letting the sun warm me, while the sounds of the gulls, and the early morning ocean waves gently caressing the sand slowly healed me. After a while, I made my way from the beach back to the street and bought a Sunday edition of the Washington Post and headed for the nearest place I could find to get some tea and toast and attempt to rejoin my body.

A local Pancake House was the closest. Unlike the Formica and plastic types that proliferate at seaside towns, it was one of the older places in the downtown resort area, dark, with warm wooden paneling and real hardwood chairs and tables. I hadn't been visiting such places for a while (I had already been a natural food and "herbal" tea guy for a long time), but I needed a quiet place and something in my stomach, quick! Sitting there, looking at some beautiful paintings done on stained wood by a very talented local artist, I began to feel almost normal again.

I was sitting in a booth alongside the far wall, facing the rear of the restaurant, lost in the Sunday double-sections of comics. Out of the corner of my eye, I noticed a group entering and seating themselves at a large table in the middle of the room. I just kept reading, not bothering to look up. If I couldn't actually *be* alone, I could at least pretend I was.

In a few minutes, someone I recognized from his work at the A.R.E. book-store, Mark Vieweg, came over to my booth and said, "Excuse me. I remember talking with you at the A.R.E. That's the Rev. Paul Solomon over there. He would like very much to meet you, and was wondering if you might care to join our table?"

Well, that was more than strange! If I had seen them first, I probably would have gone over to apologize for crawling out of his presentation. I knew that people had "come from all over" for it. I'd heard one couple had even flown over from England!

Paul was seated at the head of the two joined tables, and the others made room so I could have the seat directly to his right. After we had introduced ourselves around, Paul asked, "So, we're all curious, why did you leave just as I was coming up onstage to speak? The place was packed, everyone could see you crawling across the stage, and many of those in attendance had come great distances to hear this talk, some from out of the country. And yet, there you are, sneaking out just as I'm about to be introduced. Do you already know all you need to about such things? Do you feel that I had nothing to add to your knowledge?

"And, by the way, thank you. The music was beautiful."

I couldn't keep myself from laughing. I had yet to give any thought to what it must have looked like. At that time, I was completely engaged in self-preservation. All I was thinking as I crawled was, if I throw up right now on this carpet, it's going to ruin this day for everyone!

After I stopped laughing I began to explain how the exact same subject matter had long been my own pursuit, and that I had been eagerly looking forward to his presentation for days. I further explained how the other guy on the stage with us had just about separated me from my body forever with that incredible explosion from the Tibetan gong. I described in detail exactly what was happening to me as I was crawling off the stage, and we all laughed long and hard. When he was done laughing, Paul said I was forgiven and that he understood perfectly.

We spoke of many things, all of us eventually relating the longings that impelled us to seek beyond everyday wants and needs. There was no one at that table who did not have some version of the same desire I had, to learn as much as possible about the so-called hidden worlds. While our inspirations were unique to our own lives, our aspirations were the same. We were kindred spirits, to say the least.

Before too long, it was time for them to leave. Paul then did something I would later come to see as perhaps his signature gift. He could discern intuitively what a person might need for their growth. Or, more accurately, what the Soul desired. He would then present a doorway to that path, creating a space for that person to hear their own prompting from within and give them room to respond - or not.

He did this with absolutely no desire for a specific outcome, aside from that of an older and wiser brother wanting to help a spiritual sibling realize his or her heart's desire. He would simply create the opportunity for someone to have a spiritual growth experience, and then just observe, often with a hint of a smile. He was quietly aware that he was merely doing his part, creating a circumstance and allowing us to *choose* to awaken to our part. It is exactly what actually happens to us all every day, but in our high-speed world we are so seldom aware of it.

In my case, it went like this:

Paul: "So what's next on your musical agenda? Where do you go?"

Me: "Well, we actually don't have another performance until next weekend, so we'll probably just concentrate on healing sessions at the house. People come from all over for a personalized healing experience that we also tape for them, and Joel has us practice different musical exercises that are more like brain-integration techniques, etc."

Paul: "You know, music is my absolute favorite thing in all the world. I can't live without it. I like to put on *Godspell* and sing along really loud. In the car, it keeps me awake when I'm tired. Around the house, it's always inspirational – and motivational. But I only do it when I'm alone (laughing). Singing is not my gift this time around. It just makes me feel good. That reminds me, the tape player is broken in my car, and I've got to drive all the way to New Jersey tonight. I have a big schedule of readings to do with a doctor who helps care for my body."

Me: "Ah, New Jersey, spent a lot of time there as a child. I've got aunts and uncles in a couple of different towns, all up and down the Jersey Turnpike. We used to drive over from my home in northeastern Pennsylvania and visit them all when I was a kid. Go to the shore, etc."

Paul: "I'll be going pretty far north, around Toms River, it's called 'Bricktown'. I need to be there around noon tomorrow so I'll have to leave early this evening. I'll probably layover in Philadelphia. (pause)

"I do it fairly often. It's a long drive . . . alone. (pause)

"Especially with no music. (pause)

Me: "Yeah. It would be that's for sure."

Paul: "Radio's no help. The stations fade in and out about every 10 or 20 miles. (long pause) "Really boring..." (Really long pause)

Me: (Hesitantly), "Hmmm, maybe I could ride up with you and keep you company? We won't be able to sing along with Godspell, but at least you'll have someone to talk to. And, since I missed your actual presentation, you could do it all over again just for me!" Lots of laughter.

Paul, laughing: "You would do that?"

Me: "Sure. I haven't been 'on the road' for a while. I could hitchhike back in a couple of days. I've hitched across the country, as well as back and forth from here to my home in Pennsylvania a number of times. I love meeting people in places I never knew existed.

"I could even head over to my hometown for a day. It's just a couple hours west, since I'd be that far north, and say hello to my family and friends. I'd still have plenty of time to get back for the next gig. Plus, I've got aunts and uncles I haven't seen in a couple years all over New Jersey, so I won't have any trouble with a place to stay."

Paul: "Well, I'm sure we could find room at Dr. Kelly's for you. I was thinking, perhaps you'd like to see a reading done?"

Me: *"What?! When do we leave?"* And just like that, a lot of lives would never be the same again.

The ride itself, it seemed to me, was a perfect metaphor for that moment in our lives - he had already been where we were going, and I could hardly wait to get there. A decade of searching, trying to understand (often just survive) the circumstances of my life, finally seemed about to come to some fruition. We rode for hours, the only sounds were the hum of the highway and our quiet conversation, rising and falling turning this way and that, moving inexorably toward a shared destination. There was an easy familiarity, a more profound version of the "I know this guy from somewhere" feeling about it all.

Paul and I quickly discovered that we shared an incontrovertible (albeit painfully acquired) mutual understanding: If you ask God to liberate you from ignorance and guide you into becoming all that is intended for you, God will, (in the immortal words of John Candy, in a recurring "Second City TV" skit) "Blow you up real good!"

Nothing in our lives is 'sacred' to The One who is just trying to bring us all home.

Our groundbreaking exchange occurred when Paul sincerely offered his condolences for the early passing of my wife. We had been explaining to one another how we had come to be the kind of people we were, when he said softly and sincerely, "Michael, I have no doubt you have heard this before, but, "*He whom the Lord loveth, He chastiseth.*"

To which I quietly, and equally sincerely, replied, "Well, He obviously loveth the shit out of me." Paul burst out laughing, causing me to do the same. It quickly became one of those moments where one person's laughter causes the other to laugh harder, which then causes the first person to laugh even harder! Soon, tears were rolling down our faces. It was an enormous release! (Thank God *he* was driving.)

Like me, apparently the poor guy was only too happy to find someone with whom he could be reverently irreverent. "God's already heard it all." I heard him say more than once.

I had already garnered a reputation as a "really spiritual" guy, and he, of course, was already "Paul Solomon" - which just means that, in those *personae,* one cannot always speak plainly or completely freely.

The real Truth about a situation might actually create *more* confusion in a person who has asked you to clarify something vital to them. There are levels of understanding that must be respected and slowly grown into. The "hidden things of God" are not actually hidden from anyone. But they do require study and growth.

We both knew from experience that one must be circumspect when someone else's spiritual growth, sometimes even their sanity, is in the balance. Ironically, the very thing you are always trying to accomplish _is_ completely open communication about the things most people do <u>not</u> want to talk about – and all from the highest and deepest parts of your "self" that you are conscious of.

But, all things in their time.

Paul and I were gratefully peeling away our own layers, discovering that we also shared the scary, "Awareness That Must Not Be Spoken". It must not be spoken because, as Zen masters teach, and many people believe: "_He who knows, does not say. He who says, does not know_". (One of my favorite names for God, by the way, is "He Who".)

Be that as it may, the rational conclusion that any sane and reasoning soul (with or without a Zen master around for help) must eventually and logically arrive at, might read something like this:

"If God is <u>everything,</u> then I AM obviously a part of that infinite omnipresent whole. Indeed, for good or for ill, I AM the thinking, reasoning, co-creating, projection into matter part - of God Himself! (Whoa!)

"And, therefore, as such, I am completely justified in expecting that on some level, no matter how convoluted or ethereal, *this whole damn thing begins to make some kind of sense!*

"Also, that it is <u>good</u> to laugh, just as long and as hard as I have previously wept, at whatever I see.

"And, [<u>very</u> important, here] that some part of 'me' has been at least complicit, and probably actively participating in the creation of it all -- good *and* evil -- on a scale so grand and an arc of time so long that I cannot, at least with my finite mind, even begin to comprehend and truly know . But I AM *not* afraid to die trying!"

It soon became apparent that this former Southern Baptist Minister and I had, at least throughout our most recent years, both eagerly sought and embraced anything and everything we could find that this world had to offer (at least in terms of spiritual awakening and its peripherals) and could relate, one weary soul to another. We shared a mutual need to communicate from, and about, the very deepest parts of our selves - that would help a lot. (To this day, I am accused of "having no boundaries". But the Universal Mind, God, even the physical Universe itself has no boundaries! So how can we? And why should we pretend to?)

Our common denominator was the burning desire to know those so-called "hidden" things of God - without waiting until we were dead to experience them! And we both agreed that no God worthy of that title would want any of us, His offspring, created in His image and likeness and from His own Spirit, no less, to walk this earth terminally stupid - pitifully, even dangerously, ignorant of our very own nature.

Paul spoke openly of how frustrated he had become since the beginning of "the work", having to hear the tapes afterward in order to even know what had been spoken. Especially since the readings themselves described the Source of the information as "the very highest part of his mind, and yours." What irony, that he was the vehicle for others (like me!) to have that very conversation I had been seeking for so long, but he himself could not even be a part of it consciously.

I recall the Source describing the dynamic that occurred, in our vernacular: "Children, if you could see how silly [*silly?*] you appear from here. Having this one leave his body to commune with your own soul's record - that which lies within you, is in fact the very You of you – then, speaking through these lips those things which he retrieved from your own record, speaking them aloud into this room where they will enter your ears as sounds to be interpreted by your brain, all in order for your own experiences to become accessible to your conscious mind.

"The information and the guidance to grow from it, then, will be offered. And, quite possibly, even rejected! For it comes from without. It comes *through* another. It is, to your conscious mind, a 'reading', not a realization. It is for this reason alone that you *must* learn to access that information and guidance within you. It is the purpose of this work that you discover He who *lives* within you. It is the purpose of this Fellowship, and the only real purpose of your life! Be about it!"

I could understand Paul's frustration completely. Who has *not* longed, at some point in their life, for a real one-on-one conversation with God? Personally, I was weary to my soul of begging for answers that either didn't arrive, or I was just too stupid to decipher. However, I would learn that "The Source" had stated often that the question, and the way it was presented, determined the answer that could be brought.

By now, perhaps Paul was seeing in me someone with the same questions as he, someone who might ask them as he would. I was enjoying immensely the possibility that those questions - burning inside of me for years, and unanswerable anywhere else on earth that I was aware of - could finally be asked! And, asked of the only person that mattered, the heretofore very elusive "God".

It would eventually be made clear that inspiring those questions that were seemingly seared into my soul was the only reason - the "Soul" purpose, if you will - behind *all* of my experiences. Everything, from the tragedy of Doris' death to my boredom in High School, was designed to facilitate a search for answers most of us don't usually have the questions for – at least until we are on our *own* death beds and about to cross over. Those experiences had caused me to search for knowledge in places I had intuitively known would prove far more useful than anything I was going to learn in high school – or any other "formal" education. They had been <u>designed</u> to impel my search for understanding – and hopefully, in the words of a Cayce reading, "...the wisdom to apply same."

After renting a couple of rooms overnight at the YMCA in Philadelphia (Hey, it was the 70's!), we finally arrived at the home of Dr. William Kelly and family, rested and refreshed. And it was a good thing. There were numerous requests for readings waiting for Paul, and at that time they were pretty much all the financial income the fledgling *Fellowship of the Inner Light* had.

I had my own imaginings about what might be about to transpire, but the first time I witnessed an actual reading I quickly realized that there was no way I could possibly have been prepared for it.

To intellectually accept that someone could willingly leave their body and that it would then be used as an instrument for those in the very highest spiritual realms to speak through, is one thing: I had already read hundreds of Edgar Cayce readings and many books based upon them. But to experience such a thing, to be a part of it, united in prayer and meditation as it occurs, is quite something else.

Paul lay on his back on a small bed, shoes off, clothing loose, and recited slowly and deliberately The Lord's Prayer, invoking "the Divine Presence of Jesus, the Christ, to surround, protect, and inspire [him], and to direct the work".

(As I said earlier, one thing we can all agree on about the Christ, Jesus. You call Him, He comes. When we call upon that name, we are calling upon the all-dimensional embodiment of the very highest that is within us, and it is written, "He that is within us is greater than he that is in the world." Which would also include all our 'egos', by the way. I mention this simply to dissuade those devoutly religious souls who might dismiss this work as "satanic", hocus-pocus, or darkness of *any* kind.

"Evil" simply cannot stand the presence of the Light - the Living Presence. It is the one sure-fire way to protect ourselves – always! - from undue or unholy spiritual influence. One need only call upon the name of the Christ, Jesus [or you may use *Yeshua*, as he was actually known when in the Earth] and know that He will, in all ways and forever, protect or inspire anyone who asks. Loves it. Lives for it! Only our "self" can separate us from the Divine Love from which we were made, and even that is just an illusion - a trick of the mind. It is a biblical Truth that, "...the devils themselves believe, and tremble!")

Paul then interlaced his fingers and placed his hands across his forehead, palms outward. Next, the "suggestion" was given that would relax him completely, instructing him to release himself from his body, and find himself "...safe, and resting in the loving arms of the Divine Father." His hands came slowly down with his fingers still interlaced across his solar plexus.

Paul's breathing became shallow, his mouth fell open slightly, and he began to softly snore. In less than a minute, his body jerked as if a sudden cramp had contracted his stomach muscles, the air in his lungs was sharply and audibly expelled as he exited the body. His arms fell limply at his sides, and he lay perfectly still. It was here that I had my second shock - the first being the violence with which the body reacted to his exiting. I was shocked because I immediately recognized a lifeless body! My new friend Paul was now *dead!*

To anyone familiar with death, it was absolutely obvious there was no longer "life" in that body. He was not sleeping, he had just *been* sleeping - and snoring – now he was <u>gone</u>! There was no one in there.

There is a tangible stillness about those who are dead that cannot be imitated or faked. <u>Nothing</u> moves. There is, of course, no breath. The last breath that leaves the body causes the lungs themselves to collapse completely. There is no pulse, no movement of blood, nothing. You've no doubt heard the phrase, "deathly still". Paul's body might as well have been a softer version of one of Madame Tussaud's wax statues, lying prone. It was a corpse.

[On an *EEG* machine at Duke University's J.B. Rheine Institute, his brain waves when in trance registered first at *theta* and then *delta* while speaking "from the records".]

In a short while, there is a shudder! An intake of breath. Slowly, the head begins to move slightly back and forth, the hands come back up, cross over the solar plexus. And then, the voice:

"Yes, we are here".

The suggestion to access the specific records of the person seeking is given. Again, silence. The right index finger begins to move, almost pointing, "Yes, we have those records." The voice still has the tone or timbre of Paul's waking voice, but the manner of speaking is different, softer, but more authoritative.

Through the entire course of the reading the speech pattern is somewhat slower than Paul's waking cadence, more precise and relaxed, but unequivocal. What is spoken, simply *is*.

It was later explained to me that "they" would enter through the crown "chakra", at the top of the head, using the brain much like a bio-computer in order to operate the various functions of the body that create speech: breath, for the voice; facial and throat muscles for the formation of the words; etc.

Those who spoke through Paul at those times, referred to themselves as "...that August Body, from the beginning charged with such communication from the Throne of Grace – what you refer to as *The White Brotherhood . . .*"

These are also known, as the "Ascended Masters". Those who have, throughout time, so completely crucified "self" as to be One again with God, losing themselves in Love and service to humanity.

Right now, in that little room at the good doctor's house, even with Paul "gone", there was plenty of Life energy - brother Paul was certainly keeping the best of company!

My heart was fairly bursting at what I was witnessing. This wasn't someone sitting across a table "reading" cards, or palms, or even intuiting, no matter how accurately or sincerely. This was the eternal record of a Soul, the Akasha itself being spoken, in the context of the life today. This was access to the "Book of Life" spoken of in Revelations.

In between readings, I could barely speak to either Paul or Bill. The implications had my head spinning. Every unanswered question I had wrestled with for a decade was clamoring for attention!

More importantly, everything that I and thousands of others throughout the world – especially those already familiar with the Cayce material - had ever dreamed of was again possible! A pure, unadulterated source of unimpeachable knowledge and wisdom, about all the things we could not seem to discern ourselves. Mankind was again blest beyond measure!

The Source would describe this gathering of work as "Pure Gold".

Speaking of Gold!

That first day, the readings were all health related. Most were referrals from other physicians to Dr. Kelly. Four of the six readings given that day contained recommendations for the use of the "...Wet Cell Appliance, with gold chloride".

This is a simple device (a large version of a basic high school science experiment) consisting of a 3 to 5 gallon plastic container and a few quarts of water and other chemicals, including sulfuric acid. Two metal poles are immersed in it, and long wires lead from those terminals to two small metal plates that will be attached to the body with a gel and tape in specific places, according to the needs of the patient.

Most commonly, these are the left ankle and right wrist for a prescribed time; and then the right ankle and left wrist for an equal time. They are also applied to various spinal vertebrate, according to need.

The appliance was first designed and brought through in the Edgar Cayce readings. It creates a low-grade electrical current that is affected by a substance in a small container between the two immersed poles.

While it has been in use for over 50 years, it was not well known outside certain circles, neither is it a common need. That is why it was quite extraordinary that so many people in this one small upper New Jersey geographical area would need it, and all at the same time!

Paul asked that Bill put a "tag" question at the end of the next health reading, requesting an explanation for the repeated recommendation of the appliance.

That evening, when we resumed the readings, Bill asked why and how there could be so many people in need of this previously arcane treatment, all in this one locale, and all at this particular time.

The Source explained that it was simply time to expand man's understanding of himself as a bio-electrical being: that we, our bodies, are a combination of chemicals, trace elements and electro-magnetic energy, expressing itself in physical form. They went on to explain that at times it was necessary to "whisper in the ear" of certain individuals who had the kind of problem requiring such treatment in an attempt to guide them, to inspire them, to seek specific sources of assistance:

"Do understand, children. We do not cause these conditions, but merely attempt to influence the awareness of those whom, in the course of the working out of their own karma, might well serve the Father's greater purpose.

"This specific information is necessary at this time as man is capable of understanding the true nature of his world, the molecular and atomic vibrations even of living tissue, the body as electro-magnetic in nature. This has not been so until recently [*at least in 1975 - Author*].

"So we attempt to direct that these souls might eventually be brought into contact with this conductor, Dr. Kelly, in his normal practice. Unable to treat this effectively through usual means, he would then recommend this servant's gift of "channeling", as you refer to it, and so the information can then be given as will bring the healing. *And through the repetition, as well, generate your curiosity.*

"In these ways we make possible the increased understanding of the nature of energy and matter, even your own bodies, and the veil between worlds is made somewhat less dense for all."

So, the subjects of the readings had, in the course of seeking help for their illness, eventually found themselves seeking assistance from our Dr. Kelly; who, in turn, would then seek assistance through Paul; this would then generate our curiosity, and thus the dissemination of *new knowledge that is needed by the whole human race at this time!* Perfect!

In other words, the "attracting" of these persons, all specifically needing the wet-cell, to Dr. Kelly, was super-consciously designed, if you will, simply to generate the question we were asking. (This brings a new dimension to the biblical admonition, "Ye have not, because ye ask not!")

That question would then "open the door" for an answer that would eventually bring a very detailed explanation of the actual effect of the wet-cell appliance, and the previously unknown physical needs of the human body in this time. That is:

The human body, bio-chemically, is a mini-replica of the planet containing corresponding traces of virtually every element existing in the earth. However, our bodies have been nourished incompletely because most of our food crops are being grown without proper rotation, thus the soil is depleted of many of the essential nutrients we eat that particular food to obtain. Among these are trace elements absolutely necessary for optimum health.

Gold is an essential trace element, needed for the maintaining and operation of the central nervous system. We obtain gold for our bodies primarily from carrots and some seafood. Mega-farming techniques, lack of crop rotation, chemical substitutes for fertilizer and pest control, etc., have already altered the chemical balance of the soil and depleted much of it of natural elements, especially gold!

One result of this soil depletion has been that many of us no longer even have the molecular signature for gold imprinted in our cells! The result is that, even if one should partake of an organically grown carrot containing the proper amount of gold from a healthy soil, <u>the cells can no longer recognize the sorely needed element.</u> The body itself is no longer able to identify, digest and absorb the gold, and it simply passes through the body as waste!

The gold chloride placed between the poles of the battery terminals in the wet-cell solution, imparts the vibratory signature of gold to the electrical current. The current, flowing between the poles and thus through the body, re-establishes the molecular "signature" of the gold onto the cells. This re-establishing of the electromagnetic "signature", or gold "vibration", in the cells of the body allows them to again recognize and utilize the gold element when it becomes available, thus restoring balance to the central nervous system.

That fairly cosmic (but impeccably logical, and medically sound) explanation from the Source; and the prior 24 hours alone with Paul - culminating with the contributions of a number of very normal everyday people in physical distress *merely to assist in the evolution of the human race!* - was almost more than I could process. I could not have been more humbled if I had opened my eyes and beheld a "burning bush", instead of my very interesting new friend's still empty body.

Toward the end of the day's readings, Paul came to me and said, "I'm being told to include you in a reading. There is something they want to tell you. At the end of the next reading we will add a tag question that won't go on the clients tape, and ask what it is they would like to impart. It will have to be in the form of a specific question, so, what if we ask about our past associations, or your soul's purpose for this life? Do you have any questions in case there's time?"

I looked at him like he was crazy! My mind was screaming: *WHAT!? ME? Questions?! After everything we talked about on the way up here?*

He surely heard my screaming thoughts, because he started to laugh. (If he could see auras, as I'd heard, mine must have looked like a pin-ball machine!)

Still, even after his little joke, I could tell from the way he looked at me that something far more important than curiosity or any of my "needs" was going on. He, too, obviously wanted to know about our past together. But, just as obviously, was feeling a little unease. I didn't understand why, and he later admitted that neither did he - but he knew better than to doubt. He was seeing and feeling things I couldn't yet.

I was just kind of clueless - and very excited.

One thing I did know was that I had better be about collecting myself. It was shaping up to be quite a night. By this time in my life, I had already articulated to many others my own realization that, "It's all perfect! It just looks funny." From my perspective, God and I had finally reached the spiritual equivalent of "peaceful coexistence". Still, I would dearly love some details, just to take the edge off my still somewhat reluctant acquiescence to the way my life had played out. Paul seemed eager to help, and, yet hesitant at the same time . . . very interesting. I couldn't spend much time speculating on the apparent dichotomy, I was about to take part in a conversation I'd been waiting for all of my adult life! At least, that's what I anticipated.

After years of doing the readings, he could sense the presence of those gathering to take part in the work. I made a short list of questions, things that were of paramount importance to me.

Somewhere down the list was the one they chose to answer first without Bill even having to ask. I had written: "What prior experiences in the earth most affect and inform the purpose of this life?" I was humbled when the Source began to speak spontaneously of the time of the Christ.

My parents, in that time, were apparently among the early followers of Jesus. I was a child. In fact, one of the children with whom He had been playing the day the early disciples questioned His priorities, bringing forth the admonition, *"Except ye become again as one of these little ones, ye shall in no way enter in!"*

Much later in that life, I would become "... scribe to this channel after he became the Apostle, and transcribed those letters from Paul to the different churches, those which you have preserved even in your scripture. This one taking them from place to place, along with money from the rich churches to the poorer ones, these having all things in common, you see, as it is written."

I was told my name in that time was "Lucius", and I remembered that Edgar Cayce also had that name when Bishop of the church of Laodecia. I wondered if we had been related.

I was instructed to return to Virginia Beach: "Should return to that place of storing these [readings]. Research them, all of them. The greater understanding of the purpose in this time is to serve again. A courier from church to church, from person to person, from understanding to understanding, faithfully carrying the word, and letting it be known: The Christ lives! And His message is taught, and here is the food!

"Search that already given, all that has been given from these records. Gather here and there in specific groupings those teachings concerning subjects and make them available for research. And yet, not only here. Make them further available for publication.

"And yet, not only there: Be an ambassador, particularly to groups gathering to whom you might speak and teach, a messenger to the churches as you were in that day. Building a community of churches, as did Paul. Was developed because of his authority in that day in much that manner that you would consider now a Bishop, an overseer. His authority was recognized in the many churches. Though their pastors may be another, still they sent to him for answers to questions and such.

"Would it be again. Find those who are as sheep without a shepherd. Be a missionary in this time as you were in that. Disseminate the Word, the Gospel. *Never* glorifying the self, nor the channel, but The Word! The Word itself, that men may know."

There it was again: "The Word".

So many refer to The Bible itself as "The Word of God", without ever seeing the journey inward to the *living* Word. Instead, they end up memorizing the book! Meanwhile the Author of the Book – the Word, Itself! - is alive and well, waiting inside!

I would stay in New Jersey for one more day, watching and learning. I told Paul it was time for me to head back, as I wanted to stop by my home in Pennsylvania, about two and a half hours west, and spend a day with my family. He asked if I would deliver a note to, I believe, Sharon when I got back to Va. Beach. (Sharon was his secretary at the time, years later she would become his wife.) He also entrusted me with the money he had just received for the readings to date. Some Fellowship bills needed to be paid quickly and I would be faster than mailing it and certainly less expensive than wiring it. [That was my original take on it, but I believe he was also demonstrating to me his trust that I would serve again, unselfishly, and wanted me to experience that - knowing full well I would consider it a sacred responsibility.] He stuck in a note explaining how the money should be spent, and I put it all in my backpack and prepared to set out. The next day Bill gave me a ride to Interstate 80 and off I went, headed for the Poconos.

All Together . . . *Now!*

Getting a ride took longer than I expected. By the time I got into northeastern Pennsylvania it was already becoming dark. My last ride had to turn off of Rte. 80 well before my preferred exit, and I was left there on the local highway that eventually would run into my hometown. I stood there in the mountains for quite a long time as only a few cars came by. He had turned off of this highway onto a local road, and as far as I could see in any direction there was not a building of any kind in sight. I was stuck at this tiny intersection, deep in the Pocono Mountains. And it was now getting deep-in-the-mountains dark, with barely a car every 10 or 15 minutes. After a little more than an hour, it had become night.

The only light was from the countless stars. If I held my hand out in front of me I could only 'see' it because it blotted out the stars when I raised it up. It was like being in a "Sensory Deprivation Tank", only I was standing up. I stared off into the darkness at the silhouetted rolling mountains in the indiscernible distance. It was an extremely meditative environment, having just the starlight for any sensory stimulation, and the deep silence and utter blackness surrounding me.

As I stood there under the dim glow of the stars, gazing off into the darkness, the mountains, which were only silhouettes against the sky, began to turn a soft golden hue and slowly came into focus. The mountains were now glowing a deep starlit gold, and had become sand dunes in a desert night! Off in the distance, far across from where the mountain road had been, there appeared to be a small oasis! A few palm trees were lit from below by a small fire in the midst of it. I knew somehow that this was my destination, and that I was almost there.

Very faintly, a moving light appeared off to the left in my peripheral vision, and without turning to look I could see in my mind that it was someone carrying a lantern and they were walking ahead of a caravan, leading it to that oasis. Traveling at night, to avoid the desert heat - of course! – and using the stars for guidance. I became aware that I was wearing a long robe with a head-covering, a *burnoose*, to cover my head and neck, and I had a small bag over my shoulder. I knew there was money in it, from one of the richer churches to be brought to one of the poorer, and that there was also a letter from "Paul", advising the recipients how best to use it!

I knew that I was to meet with that caravan and proceed with them to the next town. At the very same time, I also knew I was in the middle of eternity, just doing what I knew to do in service to Life - in service to that which we call the Christ – my fellow brothers and sisters in the Light of Divine Love. It was my nature, what I knew in my Soul.

I was at both this desert crossroads and a crossroad of time! The past and present were one, absolutely indistinguishable from one another, except for the accoutrements of the era – camels or automobiles? Hand woven robes, or mass produced blue-jeans? Leather sandals, or rubber-soled sneakers? And, of course, the geographic locale.

Everything else, Life itself, was the same, and *always* was. Just behind the brain-mind everything is happening at once, in the only 'time' there really is – right Now!

I could feel the caravan getting closer, see it out of the corner of my eye. The lantern was getting brighter as it got nearer, until its light became so bright the sand dunes disappeared and the onrushing light became the single headlight of a car speeding toward me. (One headlight was out so there was only "One Light" . . . subtle!) Then it roared past, and was gone.

I stood there, unable to move. My mind easily flowing back and forth through "time", seeing, feeling, "remembering" both places at once. I was in the center of what my Hindu friends would refer to as my "dharma". I was just doing what I do, in eternity. I was both there, and here. There was no doubt in my mind that this was a prior 'experience', a 'past-life' brought to the forefront of my consciousness, given to me by the Grace of God to encourage me and assuage any lingering doubts by replicating the outer circumstances and my Soul's purpose.

The eternal Spirit in the absolute stillness of both the old deep mountains and the Sahara at night would, of course, be exactly the same. Deserts and mountains have been known throughout recorded history for their spiritual power. Mystics, Avatars, Shamans and Prophets - from Moses to Jesus, Mohammed, and more - withdrew to both environs to seek communion with the eternal unchanging Spirit. Here, a few miles from my birthplace into this life, a distant memory had intervened. Mind and Soul merged, and I was in both lives at once.

I could hardly wait to get back to Virginia Beach - to my newly remembered *real* job!

Bringing It All Back Home!

Upon arriving back in Virginia Beach, I went directly to the large home on 37th Street where the Fellowship offices and Paul's quarters were located. On the far side of the living room, above the fireplace mantel, I was stunned to see an, at least, 3 foot square painting - a perfect reproduction! - of The Light! An incredible duplication of the Light I had experienced within me!

I had found it virtually impossible to even describe, so it was inconceivable that someone would attempt to reproduce it in *any* known medium. But, there it was, almost as real as a photograph! The pastel colored clouds with sparkling gold lights like tiny stars, creating a tunnel inward to the center; the brilliant white light, pouring out in diamond-faceted geometric webs of pure coherent white-light patterns flowing forth from its center. Everything was there but the sound of the countless voices. Tears filled my eyes. If this was the "Inner Light" this "Fellowship" was all about, I was finally home!

Whoever painted it must have beheld it almost continuously as they painted, the detail was exquisite. According to the first person I spoke to, when I regained my composure, it was done by a woman known only as "Rose". This was the only subject she painted, in a variety of sizes, and she lived in a pyramid atop a mountain just outside of Atlanta. Perfect!

Paul soon returned from New Jersey and it was not long before the Source recommended that I assume the role of conductor of the readings and Paul's protégé.

"Protégé" may be a bit of a misnomer, as the Source regularly exhorted us all to rise to successive heights of spiritual awareness so that we could, and should, "teach your teacher". That in any *Guru/Chela*, - Teacher/Student relationship, there is always an equal give and take. The Christ within is the same for all. Our preconceptions of spiritual hierarchy do not apply in the evolution of Souls. Human values are of no consequence once out of the body. See: *"He that will be the greatest among you would be the servant of all.";* *"The first shall be last, and the last will be first.";* *"Know ye not that ye are Gods, and sons and daughters of the Most High?"*

A seeker once asked the Source how he might "...meet an Ascended Master?" He was told: *"If you would meet an ascended master, then become one."* Like attracts like.

Even more specifically, from a later reading:

"Do not be influenced by that which men count as valuable or successful, or achievement. That person is successful who causes happiness...and a reflection of the Divine in the lives of others. There are those on your plane who will make a great mark in history...there are those who will develop talents and abilities easily recognizable to others on your plane. Yet, not a shred of evidence of that accomplishment will be found on these records of Soul growth. For it is not that which men recognize as accomplishment, that

is recorded here as the achievement of a Soul. But that one who causes the son or daughter, the wife, the neighbor, to have a little more Light, a little more pleasure, love, energy, happiness with which to accomplish the day to day living, he has lifted himself - and the entire race – a little closer to God.

Think long and hard on that.

Any "spiritual teacher" is merely a guide and a catalyst to self-realization, and then service. True teachers readily admit that they also learn from those they teach – their 'lessons' are more subtle, but no less profound - because we are all the embodiment of God. And, we cannot find God by seeking only *within* ourselves – it is in becoming aware of God outside of self, in others, that actually allows the experience of Oneness. That is the central truth of "reality".

In the end, everyone we meet is an opportunity to both receive knowledge of ourselves and renew and enhance our relationship with our Source. And then, as our own ego-self merges back into oneness with Life itself, we truly live as an example of what is possible.

An old farmer friend once clarified for me, in his own earthy vernacular, our journey through life: "Sometimes you're The Gardener, sometimes you're the carrot." Yep!

Unbeknownst to me, at the time, I was also to become the first person to be taught the ILC Course by Paul specifically to become a teacher, although we were being informed regularly that we must all one day be "sent out from here" to share what treasures we had discovered, each in his or her own way. But, at that time, I was the one directed to accompany him "everywhere", so that we co-taught on a number of occasions. He once told me he even liked my presentation of the "Lord's Prayer Night" better than his own! To me, that was akin to winning a Grammy. And it boosted my confidence immensely, which was necessary at the time. After many years in the Baptist pulpits, Paul was a confident and gifted orator, one who quite often "channeled" consciously, especially when speaking to groups. So, at least in the beginning, he was a very intimidating presence to my (trying to be 'humble') hippy-yogi, self.

What made my presentation of The Lord's Prayer different was my previous exposure to the series of Cayce readings previously published as a study on The Book of the Revelation. For example, in explaining the attributes of each "church" it described certain predictable responses of the ego-self, as it begins opening to an increased level of energy. Also, there is a word or phrase in the Lord's Prayer that corresponds to each of the principles delineated in those individual *Seven Churches* – the seven levels of consciousness we are capable of experiencing in our individual lives. The study gives a medically and psychologically sound explanation of the attitudes and emotions one will encounter as the *Kundalini* or Life Force rises up the spine, stimulating the glands of the endocrine system and expanding the mental-emotional attributes of that particular center.

Paul and I taught together in New Jersey, Connecticut, New York City, and on Fire Island before I would be sent out into the world, just as the readings said we must all be. But, at least for the moment, my primary "job" was to keep him in a state of protective prayer during his waking hours, and to be at his side constantly; "...eating, working, playing and praying, as one!"

In that reading, describing my responsibilities, we were also told we should sleep together. The moment that suggestion was spoken, alarms went off inside me. I had not been doing this long enough to understand yet just how totally our minds and Souls were exposed to those who serve us all on the higher levels of existence once we agreed to take part in this process. So, obviously reading my mind, and seeing clearly my doubts and suspicions, the Source stated forcefully that: *"Now you will put those thoughts of homosexuality from your mind, immediately! You will learn to sleep beside this one as readily as you would sleep with the Master Himself – until that is all you can see in each other!* That was pretty unequivocal! And, it would eventually make perfect sense to me as a spiritual, or yogic, discipline. Just more culturally imposed "stuff" that had to be purified and conquered within.

"This is a spiritual endeavor and must ever be seen as such. The purpose is, as spoken of in your scripture: 'Be ye therefore of one mind in Christ Jesus.' These are not just words alluding to some nebulous metaphorical reality, but the goal of Creation itself! See how even long-married couples in your time who sleep side-by-side for years and decades will,

over time, 'finish each other's thoughts' as you say. They have become of one mind. They have become one.

"This occurs because of what you call the 'bio-energy' of your individual body-minds, visible to many on your plane as 'auras'. These individualized electro-magnetic bodies – <u>which you are</u> - will exchange that electrical energy back and forth, balancing, merging one into the other while you sleep. Each of you, also, when you leave your bodies at night, receives schooling in the very Halls of Heaven that is also shared in this way. Thus, you are creating a unified consciousness, One Mind, so that in time you will come to know each other's thoughts and needs. Thus will you grow together.

"When any two souls, expressions of God, commit to reunite and become One, for whatever purpose, they become the Whole, the One, the Source from which all has come forth. It is already understood in your world, and is the very nature of this ever-expanding Universe, this <u>physical</u> body of God, that 'the whole is greater than just the sum of its parts'. Again, it is the merging of the divine energies <u>that you are</u> while in this world, the harmonizing of your 'separate' selves - that is the real goal, even of Life itself. "

And so it began.

I had my familiarity with the Cayce readings to prepare myself for what I could only imagine lay ahead. Paul had earlier mentioned that he had been instructed by "The Source" to go to the A.R.E. and study the work already gathered there in order to better understand what was happening to him.

Of course, as a genuine Southern Baptist Minister, the Source might as well have told him to go purchase a *Ouija* board or attend a *séance,* as to send him to Edgar Cayce's work. There was zero tolerance for such things in the fundamentalist tradition of his youth. Paul had been taught, and had believed all of his life, that such things were "of the Devil", "Satanic". To say that he was a conflicted man by the time we met would be a huge understatement.

I could not begin to imagine what he must have endured to come to the place where he could completely surrender his mind and body in this manner. When all of this happened to him, his only formal spiritual training had been at a Baptist Bible College! In other words, he had only his profound and undying faith that Jesus would watch over him and protect him when he called upon Him, invoking His presence. This much he was absolutely sure of - when you called the Master, He came!

No equivocation. No, "I don't approve" of your diet, or clothes, or job, or past, or any of the things we humans judge each other by that keep us from loving each other, and ourselves - and, we erroneously believe, even from the Love of God. When you ask Him to surround and protect you, to inspire you, to live in and through you, He does! Anybody! Right now! Because we are Him, and He knows it and we don't, yet.

The problem we humans have is that the agenda of the Christ within us is usually not at all like our own. Perhaps it would be more accurate to say that our agenda is not exactly Christ-like. While we share the same goal - "happiness" and a fruitful life for ourselves and our loved ones - we have very different ideas of how to achieve that state. So, when we call upon The Highest Within, we are usually seeking to be rescued from some craziness we've already created, or to have some seemingly dire need met or desire fulfilled, again - - whereas, God seeks only our awakening. Ironically, and comically, that very awakening is usually best facilitated *by the very circumstances we are trying so desperately to avoid!*

What to do? In the end, it's all about surrender. As the apostle Paul said: "I die daily." [1 Cr 15:31] We may not be able to go into full-trance for a reading (and why would you want to?) but we can certainly stop and look at what we have created - through the eyes of our soul. Perhaps with our own spiritual eyes we can discern if our present efforts have truly been in our own best interest.

I was beginning to appreciate the humor in the situation. Everyone who has ever read the Cayce material has had one question: Where is there another person to do such things? Why only this one man?

That Edgar's apparent successor would arrive as a, "...*genuine, buckle-of-the-Bible-belt, Southern*

Baptist Minister, John Wayne in a cleric's collar...",
only proved once again that God has what can only
be called a 'transcendent' sense of humor.

It seems Paul was not the best judge of what it
took to nourish himself, and used only his own
feelings of the moment to determine what effect the
work, and his diet (such as it was), might have on his
body. And he took his body to the limits, almost
daily.

He not only did the readings, (four or six in a
day!) but travelled extensively teaching the Inner
Light Consciousness Course. He lectured, usually as
keynote speaker, around the country, and spent any
time not doing those things (fiscally essential to the
survival of the budding Fellowship of the Inner Light)
personally answering most correspondence, while
also creating the manuals that would one day be
used by ILC teachers and students to come.

But Paul was also a genuine Southern Baptist
Minister (with the emphasis on "southern"), who had
trained as a chef when he temporarily left the
ministry during his own dark night of the soul. And,
oh, how he loved good ol' southern cooking,
especially if it might also have a New Orleans flavor
(where he had studied the culinary arts).
Consequently, Paul desperately needed someone like
Dr. Kelly to help repair the damage he would inflict
on himself regularly. And that was why he wanted
Bill to be his personal assistant and conductor, and
thus was not at all happy that the Source requested
otherwise. For a short time after the reading
suggesting I should be that person, there was some

unspoken but obvious resentment about this directive "from on high". But Paul, as most of us, had already learned that surrender was the best option.

Anyone who had been involved with "the work" for any significant period of time is well aware that the karma for seeking advice from the Source, and then not accepting the suggested course, was usually swift and unmistakable. Not 'punishment', not ever. More like: 'If that's what you prefer, despite asking for and receiving our advice, we cannot assist you."

I remember the Source saying clearly to a longstanding member of the Fellowship, "...but, suit yourself - and you will!" Apparently, with God it's pretty much: "Don't ask, if you don't want to know."

And that is the exact reason such guidance must come from within us. You can get a "reading", even the soundest advice from your very best friend (which is essentially what a real reading is), and still set it aside, ignoring the advice for any number of "good" reasons. It happens every day. But that which comes to us as a realization, has, by definition, already enlightened the ego-mind and reunited with it. No small victory!

As for my role as inspiration to a healthier lifestyle? In Paul's words (albeit, pronounced with some great love and affection) I was still "...just a rice and veggie eatin' hippie yogi, who's been living in denial."

Perhaps. Then one day, while walking down a hall in the Pierre Hotel in New York, he watched us go by in a mirror and wondered aloud to me, "How come you're only four years younger than me, and we look like father and son?" , and we did. I was 33 and looked 23, and he was 37 but looked at least 47. No one, not even Paul himself, understood that it was not just my good genes and yogic life choices. It was that the readings themselves were taking a terrible toll on his body.

I would learn that the release of his soul from the body, as the animating and life-giving presence, meant that, without him in it the body was only surviving on the residual energy left in the cells when he was in a trance. Just as an automobile will still run for a while on the power left in the battery when the alternator fails or a belt breaks. If it's at night and the headlights are on, you can watch them slowly dim while driving. In a short time, the battery will be completely drained, the lights will go out, and the car eventually "dies".

Paul's body was exactly like that, when in the trance state. The Soul, the energy we knew as Paul, would exit from the body through the solar plexus center (or *chakra*). "The Brotherhood" of those that are sent whenever heartfelt prayer is offered up to God – and dedicated throughout eternity to these specific purposes - would enter through the crown *chakra* at the top of the skull. They would then manipulate the physical body using the brain as a kind of bio-computer (which it essentially is) in order to communicate. While this was happening, all the normal physical functions had virtually stopped, and the body would begin to grow cold since there was no life force, no Soul, in it - no "Paul" - the residual energy left in the cells would begin to slowly dissipate.

As we became more harmonized, and a reading went longer than 40 minutes or so, the Source would ask me to place my fingertips on the soles of his feet and breathe in deeply and slowly of what's called the "prana" - the Light, the Life, that *is* God - in the air all around us, while also visualizing light entering in through the top of my head and expanding in my chest, my heart center (or *chakra*), filling my upper body with white light.

Then I was to "see" that light flowing from the center of my chest, down my arms and hands and into his feet, filling his body. After a few minutes of this exchange, I would be directed to continue.

It was explained to me that had we not done this, *rigor mortis* would have set in - and Paul would not have been able to re-enter his body!

What this actually meant, was: the man we knew as Paul was already *<u>physically dead</u>*, for a good portion of his life! At least three hours and often more, virtually every day! For as much as a quarter of any given day, Paul was as dead as anyone already buried in a cemetery.

No surprise, then, that when he would awaken after a reading, he would feel extremely cold and always had to have a hot cup of instant coffee waiting for him, no matter how warm the room itself actually was. And no wonder he was aging so much more rapidly than I.

Sometimes he would not get all the way back, a part of his conscious awareness still "there". Once he awoke from a reading and after sitting up and slowly swinging his legs over the edge of the small bed we used in the middle of the room, as I made him the hot instant coffee, he looked agitatedly around and angrily said, "Damn it, Michael! I told you that you must *never* allow anyone to enter this room once a reading has begun! Not under any circumstances! Who are these people? What are they doing here?" I had to calmly explain that they were not actually "here". That he was still seeing those who had gathered on the inner planes to be of assistance.

According to their own description, there was often "a cloud of witnesses" gathered to serve, including those members of the White Brotherhood whose specific purpose was this particular means of communication between the planes of existence.

Each of us, as individual Souls, have touched so many others from the beginning of Creation. And all come forth when the call goes out to assist in the most important experience of Life, on all levels – the reading of a soul's record. The returning to oneness with its Source, of a Soul seeking Truth - any Soul!

All are One in this Omni-Dimensional Holographic Universe, and the dance of the Spirit of God is not complete until *everyone* has been awakened to remembrance, and returned to oneness. (Remember, He would leave the ninety-and-nine to go in search of the one who is lost. Luke 15:4) Thus, *the highest labor of love that anyone can perform* is the assisting of <u>any</u> other of our fellow humans into the awareness of their Source - their own true nature!

Thus, in the words of the readings, "We rush to assist any time a call is heard - a cloud of witnesses, sent in answer to the seeking of any of God's children. There is no greater service, either in your world or ours, nor in all the infinite realms of Spirit."

The first time it happened to me there were only those few visible to him, and it was eerie as he began to describe what he was seeing. Later, we were told to understand and accept that this is the way it *always* is, even in our daily lives. It is well for us to remember that there are those who give themselves in service to us gladly, each and every one of us, because they see us as the very embodiment of God. And they know us and accept us as a part of themselves, and so rush to assist <u>whenever we ask</u>. Understand, that no one on any plane of existence is allowed to interfere with another soul's life path, <u>unless asked</u>! *"Ye have not, because ye ask not."* However, whenever called, they rush to assist - to serve the One. The Truth is some almost never leave our side, unless we venture into truly dark realms of selfishness, denying them spiritual fellowship, and access to our hearts. Still, there is a serious downside to recognizing them in the same way we see each other.

One night Paul was stricken with agonizing pain in his stomach area, originating in the pancreas, it turned out. The pain was so severe that he asked me to say the words that would bring about the trance state, and to immediately ask for one "Doctor Christopher". This was apparently an entity who had previously identified himself in the beginning of Paul's awakening, before we had met, when the Source was still attempting to explain exactly what was happening to this devout Southern Baptist Minister.

We were alone at home and, I'm sad to say, it was one of those few readings that were not recorded. Those were always the type either seeking personal assistance when Paul was ill, or the few times the Source requested we turn off the recorders because the information was for my, or our, ears only.

It occurred at least one other time that I'm aware of, when a professor of eastern studies was given a meditation technique that was for him only. A technique, it was explained, that would have been very dangerous to others, although it was fine for him because of his years of meditation and long practice of Kundalini Yoga.

Anxiously following Paul's request, we said the Lord's Prayer as always and Paul lay down as I gave the "suggestion", speaking the words that would have him "resting in the arms of the Divine Father, the body surrounded, protected and inspired by the Living Christ, Jesus". Paul almost immediately began the normal light snoring, and entered the deeper levels of sleep. As I saw the quick convulsion and then collapse of his body that signaled his leaving, I asked if I could "speak with Dr. Christopher about the physical state of the channel's body."

There was a much longer than usual pause as Paul's now empty body lay perfectly still. Then suddenly the body moved sharply. The head moving side to side, small, slight movements of the arms, ending with the hands folded across the stomach, the index finger on the right hand lifting upward, and then the voice that was Paul's, but not Paul, and the familiar, "Yes, we have this body."

Then, forcefully, angrily: *"Now, children! Never, ever, <u>ever</u> call any of us here by name! It is your own petty preoccupation with personal identity that is precisely the source of all of your problems!* (Divine alliteration!)

"We, here, seek only to serve God, even the Father, in loving service to Him who is the Author and Finisher of all Life. The Alpha and Omega, The Beginning and The End.

"You must always address your needs to Him! Always! And ask Him, who knows your every need before you even ask! And we will rejoice to be chosen to be sent! And we will rush to serve. We are blest to serve Him, by serving you! You, who are His children, His expression. We serve the Living God and in this service we too lose ourselves, becoming one again with Him. That is the only purpose of your lives, and ours, in eternity!

(long silence)

"Now, as for this channel. We are having some difficulty entering and leaving this body. We would have this one lose some ten pounds or more of excess tissue from around the solar plexus area. A five to seven ounce glass of grapefruit juice should be had every time food is taken. Then, regardless of the meal, tissue will be reduced to liquid and passed from the body. This can and must be done gently, through the diet, so as not to physically traumatize the already affected organs with what is much needed exercise, physical exertion - which must come later.

"Fried foods, especially, and sweets using refined sugars, must be completely eliminated until such time as this goal has been met. This one must learn that the body needs be respected as the temple it is, and treated as such. The repeated rapid fluctuations in the blood-sugar are causing the obvious dis-ease in the pancreas. Because of this behavior, the pancreas has become inflamed, and is the source of the pain. The discomfort will disappear with the cessation of the over-stimulation of this gland."

The reading went on with detailed instructions for me to *"...attempt to inspire the channel to learn to care for his body and see the counter-productive, even self-destructive nature of his dietary choices."* I was to keep him surrounded with Light through constant prayer, remaining aware at all times that there were those who would attempt to influence him from inner planes, seeking to direct his very thoughts and desires and then attaching themselves to his aura where they might also experience his pleasures vicariously.

Some, far more devious, are willing to do anything that might prevent the awakening of mankind to the Light, including preventing this channel from contributing his gift to the true "Second Coming" - the techniques for the awakening of humankind to its actual spiritual nature, *The Inner Light Consciousness Course.* All of us, awake and aware, are "branches of the Vine." The 'others' are shadows, and the coming of the Light means their demise, and they know it.

The reading was long and involved and this was the very first time I was instructed to place my fingers at the soles of his feet and "recharge" the body so they could continue. There was healing able to be performed from "over there" (surely on the sub-atomic and molecular level of the affected cells) restoring some semblance of balance while Paul was absent from the body.

When he awoke, feeling "refreshed and invigorated" (which was always a part of the suggestion to bring him back into his body) the pain was completely gone and he felt so good that he insisted -- *even after I told him everything that had just happened!* -- that we "...go get some fried chicken, and a decadent dessert at *The Jewish Mother* to celebrate!"

Thus was I introduced to the adventure that was going to be my life with Paul Solomon. And the reason *everything* had happened in my life was about to be shown to us both.

Oh, My God!

There are those of us who throughout the ages are familiar with this work - the bringing of "new" spiritual knowledge, the Truth, into this world by way of such communications. We all come to it quite naturally. You don't usually know you are one of these until one day you are exposed to some form of the work, and the recognition comes, and you smack your forehead and go, "Yes! Of course! I _knew_ it!"

As I said earlier, sometimes we are here in this world, on this "side", and sometimes we assist from "over there". We are all, every one of us, a spiritual family. We are One. With or without a body, our true nature never changes.

"The Work" is only about the awakening of every soul (but especially your own!), to its true nature and life's purpose. Personal accomplishments, ego identities, are of no account. They are merely fuel for the journey back to the Inner Light. "*Grist for the Mill*", brother Ram Dass titled a book about it.

Most of the situations and conditions we find ourselves in have their genesis in some long forgotten past. As we know, attitudes and emotions, choices and behaviors even in our maturity have their roots in our former experiences, whether our own childhood experiences or eons ago.

Be that as it may, through whatever depth of association we use to begin to notice the "cause & effect" nature of our lives, and must eventually admit that we are indeed reaping what we ourselves have sewn. The most important product of that realization is: we become more truly human. As we begin to acknowledge the oneness of all Life, and accept that we are the creators of our own personal lives, we quite naturally become more forgiving and patient with ourselves and others.

[There is a wonderful 'one-liner', apropos to the "Holiday Season" I am writing this portion in, comparing the Old Testament God of vengeance and retribution to the New Testament God of Love and Forgiveness. It goes: *"God has become a lot more forgiving since He became a human for a while."*]

Fortunately, we eventually realize that all of the "bad" things we have perpetrated on ourselves and others were simply done in ignorance – ignorance of the nature of Life – and that they will all someday be healed by assimilating the hard-earned wisdom. Nothing alters one's path through life quite so irrevocably as accepting the evidence, even if acquired from a book, such as *Many Mansions* (or this one) that there actually is a "plan"! A plan designed to illuminate the process by which *we* have been co-creating every circumstance in our lives for far longer than we can even remember.

Which brings us back to Doris - and my *"Honeymoon from Hell."*

The true scope of my expanding reality, courtesy of my exposure to the Cayce/Solomon readings, was finally made unmistakably clear in the reading Paul and I did, simply to ascertain the precise moment of our individual birth-times for a natal-chart overlay and comparison.

We were merely trying to get to know more about each other in the spiritual sense. If we were called by God/Source to do this thing together, we would need all the relevant info we could gather. Two more disparate individuals could hardly have been called to oneness, as far as either of us could tell. What was about to happen, though, was going to change the way we both perceived *everything!* It is the single most powerful revelation I have ever experienced, bar none, illuminating not just past-lives, but childhood visions and fantasies across the span of my youth and young adulthood. I saw *exactly,* and unmistakably, how God - Life! - is "talking to us", all the time. Especially in the parts that hurt like hell!

I was completely unaware of my exact birth-time, and Paul only knew what he had been told by hospital records from the 1930's, which were universally acknowledged to be imprecise (certainly by cosmic standards), so this was essential. Planets and stars are moving at ridiculous speeds and just a few minutes can bring an entirely different influence upon our consciousness.

Immediately, the Source revealed that Paul had been born *"...at 7 AM, on the morning of the seventh day of the seventh month, so that those who have eyes will see."* The 7-7-7 configuration is of great significance to those who understand the rhythms and harmonies inherent in the patterns of our lives.

As the Source was revealing to me the exact moment of Paul's birth, I remember thinking amusedly, "Interesting, Doris' birthday was July 8th, the day after our wedding, and we had to get her parent's permission because we were to be married the day *before* she would turn eighteen. Funny."

Wait a minute!

What!?

That means we were married on Paul Solomon's birthday?

Paul's 7/ 7/ 7 birthday was our Wedding day?

We had never gotten to celebrate even our first anniversary, so our wedding date had not been very prominent in my mind. Until now! Paul's auspicious birthday was the day Doris and I were married!

And then I remembered her family's home address, where we had spent many of our first nights curled up under blankets on the living room floor:

"1 SOLOMON Street!"

What!!!???

We were married on Paul Solomon's 777 birthday and her home was <u>1 Solomon Street</u>!?

The nightmare I had been walking around in for a decade had been a set-up?! Planned? Before we were even born!? That bloody horror that erased my whole identity had been agreed upon before we even came to Earth!?

Slowly, I began to remember why we fell in love in the first place - *everyone fell in love with her!* Even my tough-as-nails, recently discharged from the Marines cousin, Jim, came home every day after work in a shoe factory talking about this girl who was "...so cute, so nice, you just want to be around her. Sometimes when they walk by, I pretend I'm going to trip them just to get their attention. But they keep going." (Macho!) He convinced me I should come have lunch with him at the shoe factory just so I could see her and her sister. I tried, twice, but both times she did not come in. I did see her sister, and, yes, she was very pretty. I never got to meet "the younger one", but Jim would tell me about the things they did as he observed them virtually every day. Not an obsession, but he obviously was attracted to them but was clueless about ever seeing them outside the shoe factory they all worked at.

Months had gone by when I went roller-skating, across the river in another town, and I saw a girl I could not take my eyes off.

I, too, was so very shy and socially inept that all I could do was skate around in giant circles and watch her from afar, until closing.

Realizing I might never see her again, I approached her as we were all taking off our skates and exiting and said something like, "I hope I'm not bothering you, but I couldn't help but notice you, and I was wondering if I might call you sometime so we could talk, and maybe do something like this together?" She eventually gave me her number as they were leaving, and after a long phone conversation she agreed to come to my family's home and observe my cousin Jim and I making music. Jim was learning guitar and I was learning drums. In the phone conversation I told her all about how Jim and I grew up together as best friends all of our lives, and were considered by the rest of our families as the 'strange' ones. She laughed said she couldn't wait to meet him. (I understand now that we shared an artistic sensibility, and sensitivity, but were born into a family that did not recognize even the existence of such a thing.) When I got to tell Jim about her I said, "Never mind the girl from your work! This girl is just so wonderful to be with and just talk to, there's something about her I can't explain, but I just love being near her, even on the phone. You'll see."

When she arrived I went out to meet her, I explained again that Jim and I were very close and were considered the really odd one's in the family. As we approached the front door, I was hoping to myself that they could get to know each other and would enjoy each other as much as I enjoyed both of them.

As I opened the door they both looked at each other, wide-eyed with shock, and said simultaneously, "You!" She said, "*This* is your cousin and best friend?!" Jim said, "Michael! This is her, the girl from the factory that I've been telling you about everyday!" And they both burst out laughing. Destiny!

She actually *was* love incarnate. Angelic. Not a classically physical "beauty", but very pretty, soft-spoken and shy. But her eyes! When she looked at you, she seemed to look right into you in a way that filled you with a deep warmth. Of course, I wanted to be near her. Everybody did!

I realized in that moment of clarity conducting that reading, as I was being shown the life we had lived and planned so long before, that she was a "Christed Soul". A *Bhodisattva*. A being of complete love and compassion. One who comes to this earth not because *they* need to be here – but because *we* need them to be here. She had come to do this. Not for me, for the world. She was The Christ (just as we are <u>all</u> The Christ, branches of the vine). And she embodied, and then sacrificed, an earthly life so that I would be driven by the unrelenting confusion to seek people, places, and experiences I most definitely would *not* have as a State Trooper, or in any other "normal" role I might assume in this life.

A memory of a childhood fixation with Guillotines floated up from the depths of my subconscious. I had even created one out of clay and a discarded single edge razor-blade, and some window screen "runners" - along with little clay people! My God, what had I been responsible for in some long ago time - that I eventually had to experience that horror, the mind-shattering heart-break and loss of any sense of reality.

In the middle of the reading that I was supposed to be taking notes about and paying close attention to, I became dizzy. I even thought I might pass out. My head was spinning and I was physically faint, trying to comprehend how these events from across God only knew how much time, had all been woven into my life, culminating right there and then, in that room, with that sleeping man – and with my eternal Spirit family speaking through his body.

Oh! My God!

The "accident"! The nightmarish manner of her death, all that pain - the hopelessness, and the helpless confusion of the ensuing years - all had been designed to bring me *here*? To *this* moment? Not just physically, but mentally, emotionally and spiritually! I had been impelled – no, <u>compelled</u> – to spend a complete decade of my life seeking only this pure conversation with God!

The weaving together of those circumstances and the life that would later come from them, made it impossible to mistake the significance of what was occurring - or its importance to the greater world.

In one of the earliest recorded readings given before Paul even came to Virginia Beach, the Source emphatically told him, along with those who were the very first attempting to understand what was happening to their good friend "Bill Dove", that they must approach this work with open and contrite hearts, and great reverence. Paul said that prior to that moment they had been more like children struggling to understand a new toy, asking questions from their own admitted ignorance (after all, Paul's friend Harry had only been using hypnosis in an attempt to help Paul quit smoking when he was coming out of his own 'dark night'), when they were admonished to fast, pray, read the Bible, and meditate on the "holiness" of it all:

"Blood has been shed for your awakening, lives have been given to bring this information to you in this time!"

The Source was obviously speaking of the sacrifice of not only the Christ Jesus, but the many earlier Christians who had been burned at the stake, fed to lions, imprisoned, tortured, stoned to death or crucified - to say nothing of the acknowledged martyred saints of all faiths throughout history. But it was far more personal than that to me. And I would never be able to look at any occurrence in my life as "random" again.

If what I had experienced could be so perfectly arranged, from even before my birth, absolutely anything was - and is! – possible. I had to immediately surrender every notion I had ever entertained of what my life might actually be for and about – and never again take any moment or situation for granted. Daily life, lived multi-dimensionally, is more outrageously bizarre, deceptively simple and spiritually fulfilling, than any world saving fantasy we could ever dream up for ourselves - guaranteed!

Now What?

For an understanding of the simplicity of such a spiritually effective and fulfilling daily life, there is this: In a reading for a life-long Buddhist in Japan, the Source, illuminating the practical nature and true meaning of the Buddha's teachings, explained:

"Buddha spoke, 'Refrain from all forms of evil' - "evil" meaning any act that decreases Life or liveliness in self or others - and refrain from doing harm.

"Secondly, do all the good that you can find to do: whatever is set before you which will be of help and assistance to self and others, including healing, teaching, giving to others. And third: 'Be of a joyous, joyful spirit.' Thus the Lord Buddha has commanded that those who would follow his philosophy should be a joyous and peaceful people.

"Enjoy Life, refrain from harm, do all good and be filled with joy, Light, laughter and Truth. One who practices these simple tenants will find that enlightenment itself is quite natural.

"It is the <u>normal</u> state of any human! <u>It is unnatural to be unenlightened</u>. It is simply natural - the nature of man - to be enlightened!

"And, <u>all would be enlightened</u>, were it not for the forces of influence in early childhood which separate the parts of the world into categories: good

and bad, right and wrong, good and evil. This imposed duality has caused the consciousness to divide itself into the cleft brain of your species."

It is testimony to the difficulty of such a path (dying daily to self) that so few are actually known for accomplishing this. It requires a complete and conscious effort to set aside the "ego-self" in ways most people have never entertained the concept of, let alone actually attempted. Exactly what part of the "self" is it that must be set aside? One reading actually described it precisely, calling it - "the appetite self". Think about it. What is it that even the Buddha articulated as the source of all problems? Thus spoke the Buddha: "Desire is the cause of *all* suffering." The desire for anything from food to possessions, people, experiences, etc.

Of course, that will eventually include even the 'desire' to know God, who is invisible to us only because we refuse to acknowledge the obvious. The final relaxing into the realization of "That Which Is" is a surrender rather than an accomplishment.

There is a wonderful reversal of perspective happening in the world as I write this. As children, most of were admonished by our parents "Don't just sit there, do something!" Recently I was sent a card with a photo of a sitting Buddha. The caption read, *"Don't just do something, sit there."* Inside was: *"Be still, and know that I AM God." Ps. 46 vs 10*

I mean, really. Where else could God possibly be, being truly GOD, if not everywhere, all around us - and <u>in</u> us, as us!

The whole purpose of the march of the ages, the evolution of both our planet and the human species - not just physically, but mentally, spiritually, and emotionally - was to create and perfect a vehicle in which could dwell, eventually, without a sense of loss of divine nature: the only begotten of the Father, the Sons and Daughters of God, the children of the Light.

So, while this had all the promise of everything the Cayce readings spoke about, Paul was quick to point out that no matter how convenient it appeared to be to get any answer needed to solve any problem, it was only by teaching others to access that same Source that his soul's purpose would be fulfilled.

Hence, *"The Inner Light Consciousness Course - A guided experience in spiritual awakening."*

We have come to the time when we must all learn to hear the voice of the highest within us – the God within. And, learn to embrace the mental, physical, and spiritual disciplines necessary to allow the Power that creates galaxies with a mere thought to be heard, to manifest deep within us, and then be allowed to live *through* us. That is the true gift of Paul Solomon's work, and life.

"And in the end . . ."

Saul of Taurus, before becoming the apostle of the Christ, was a "Hebrew of the Hebrews" - "*circumcised on the eighth day*" [Phil. 3:5] - who had studied under the historically noted and highly respected Rabbi Gamaliel. But Saul was not just a learned and devout Jewish man. He was a man of the world as well, a Roman Citizen and a man of letters.

Paradoxically, before his unexpected encounter with the Christ on the road to Damascus, Saul was already infamous as a fierce persecutor of the early Christians, causing many to be imprisoned and others stoned to death.

But, God has His ways. *Saul of Tarsus* became *Paul, the Apostle*, the man whose personal experience of the Living Word famously transformed his heart and mind, ultimately changing the lives and destinies of countless Souls, from his time to ours.

It is he, whom, in his letters to the early Christian communities and church leaders, helped spread the message of the *Living God of Love* around the world, even across time itself. From that day to this, his epistles to the various disciples and early churches have changed and illumined the hearts and minds of millions - probably *billions!* - of souls, from everyday people on every continent to world leaders in their respective times.

In every nation, culture and religious affiliation, his teachings have informed the hearts of spiritual seekers everywhere in virtually every language. At the very moment you are reading this, his epistles are also being read - *and accepted as God's own words* - by men, women and children around the world seeking comfort, enlightenment, inspiration and wisdom.

In 1939, the Reverend William Dove was born into the fourth generation of a family of Southern Baptist preachers. According to his Birth Certificate, he was born at 7 am, on the 7th day of the 7th month, "So that those who have eyes might see". This was verified in the reading I conducted to ascertain our birth times in order to have our astrological charts drawn up and overlaid.

From the beginning, he was destined to have experiences that would rival even that earlier life. When he became spiritually awakened, he was told by the Source to adopt this new name, Paul Solomon, in order to symbolize the death of the old man and the birth of the new. The name would also symbolize the unity of both the Old and the New Testaments of our Bible - the divinely inspired wisdom teachings of Solomon, and the practical applications in the exhortations of Paul.

The combining of those two names was to facilitate an expanded awareness - a growth in consciousness for himself and others – and it would signal the personal spiritual rebirth of this Fundamentalist Baptist Minister into the most important "prophet", spiritual teacher, psychic, gifted orator, and explainer of the nature of God and Man to walk this Earth in many a day.

As I mentioned before, such men as he and Edgar Cayce, along with the "prophets of old" of every faith, have *always* been here - a small number of both men and women at any one time, and in every culture. Beyond the confines of any religion, they have all continually brought and updated the knowledge and wisdom of Spirit to those of us here on Earth. As the awareness of our own true nature, and the multi-dimensional nature of Creation itself, slowly becomes assimilated through our experiences and our seeking, we will see the healing of humanity. (There is no way to "game" a system that simply reflects back to you your own thoughts.)

Edgar Cayce and Paul Solomon were simply the first of the divinely inspired Prophets not limited to animal skins or hand-written parchment to record their writings. They were among the earliest beneficiaries of existing in the world when "mass communication" came of age.

Industrially produced writing paper allowed correspondence to be delivered to others virtually anywhere on earth, initially by horseback and such and later on trains, across oceans on ships, and soon afterward, Air-Mail. Newspapers and magazines would eventually make the printed word commonplace. The Telegraph would almost instantly connect even far-off continents. Soon radio and television, combined with satellites, would bring the world 'live' into people's homes – and now, the internet!

During Cayce's lifetime, it still took hours or days to span the globe. Today, *any event or idea can be shared with the whole of humanity in seconds!*

So this Soul's return in our time to serve again as messenger and teacher of Universal Truth - the very Laws and *Light* of God - bears witness to the importance of the times in which we live.

This moment is the turning of an age, just as it was two-thousand years ago when Jesus (Yeshua) completely surrendered "self" to become the Christ, and demonstrated the transformative consciousness of the *Living Light*, available within every individual. It is also 26,000 years from the time of an earlier epoch wherein the human/physical vehicle was perfected for the embodiment of our souls. This is known as the Atlantean age.

Our current day is the time for the "spiritualizing" of the conscious mind; the reunification of the brain hemispheres and the transcendence of the sense of separation - the illusion of "us and them" that is, and has been, the root cause of all strife everywhere throughout time.

All of these things are explained and clarified in the work that came through Paul, and, if you peruse prophetic discourses through the centuries, you will find that the only thing that actually changes is the vernacular - the ability of a language to describe the infinite multi-dimensional reality we actually inhabit. The discourses that came through Paul illuminate and expound on virtually all known spiritual disciplines (including, of course, both the Old and New Testament biblical teachings) and give clearly detailed explanations of recent and relevant scientific findings regarding the human condition, and our own individual potential.

Paul Solomon was a person much like the rest of us – except that he was also part of a seamless procession of actual "Prophets" that began not long ago, relatively speaking, after our descent into corporeal matter. He was also the return of the Apostle Paul (with his own karma) as spoken of in the Cayce readings. In response to a question for guidance in an early "Work Reading", asking the Source who should be the leader or director of the fledgling *Association for Research and Enlightenment,* as well as how that person might be chosen, there cam this answer:

"The leader will be that one through whom the information comes, whether Edgar Cayce or others that may be chosen to carry on - as Paul will enter in with the work." (EC. 254-53).

Some 50 years later:

"Let those who have doubts, whatever their doubts may be, let them know that there is here a fulfilling of a prophecy. That Edgar Cayce planted a seed and blazed a trail, and said clearly, 'Paul will enter the work.' Paul has entered the work! And, for a specific purpose: Edgar Cayce introduced to the world, in a magnificent way, the possibility that man can set aside completely his own

consciousness, his own mind and opinions, and be a channel for the Divine. The next step in that work is that one should come, as Paul has come, to say to others: 'You also have access to your Source. It is not for just one, and not for all.'

"It is not the case that every man can set aside his consciousness so completely as to be unconscious in trance. Only those who have completely overcome the fear of death can enter such a trance, setting aside the mind.

"And yet, anyone of you can learn, through careful application of Inner Light Consciousness, to set aside the mind sufficiently to communicate with the Source - and to do that clearly!

But the way was shone, the trail was blazed, the seed was planted, by the prophet, Edgar Cayce."
(FIL Work Rdg. 7/30/91

Throughout the ages, and from whatever time: <u>Truth *never* disagrees with itself.</u>

The explanations of our problems, whether individual or international, as well as the solutions offered, emphatically embrace the expansion of our own abilities to access previously "unseen" worlds - and unknown parts of ourselves. Scientific breakthroughs in the fields of quantum-physics and molecular medicine, coupled with the increased understanding of the effects of thought on physical matter (<u>especially our own bodies</u>!) have opened the door to a synthesis of science and spiritual understanding heretofore unknown in recorded history.

It is no secret these days that our thoughts inevitably create our reality. Indeed, have already created <u>everything</u> we have ever experienced throughout our lives. As the Buddha said:

"All that we are, is the result of what we have thought. The mind is everything. What we think, we will become."

Cayce phrased it as: *"Thoughts are things: Spirit is the power, mind is the builder, the physical is the result."*

Obviously, the ability to consciously create through visualization is the single most powerful attribute of any human being. It is what we do even when we *un*-consciously "think", cogitate, hope and dream. And, it is exactly what we are doing when we worry – <u>un-</u>consciously creating self-fulfilling prophecies. Worry is simply negative prayer – but, <u>it is equally potent</u>! To save our own lives, and our world, we absolutely must become conscious of this process and begin to take control.

Through Paul, the Source offered a meditation-visualization technique entitled *Inner Light Consciousness (ILC)*. It was first described in a reading as "A guided experience in Spiritual Evolution" - and further:

". . . as clear, practical, and unadulterated a technique for the unfolding of the human soul, the human psyche, as ever partaken! It is as potent as

<u>any</u> technique taught in <u>any</u> 'Mystery School', whether exoteric or esoteric, wherever it may be."

Obviously, this is a grand and glorious time to be alive! *If* you know what is actually taking place. Approaching the dawn of the highly anticipated "New Age", the minds of people everywhere are being prepared to rejoin their Source. Around the world in every culture, the oneness of humankind, <u>of Life itself</u>, is being recognized by all but the most entrenched ego-centric and fear driven.

It is the time for the conscious mind – described as "a wonderful servant, and a terrible master" – to be employed to bridge the hemispheres of the brain, so that the divided minds of individuals can be reunified and perfected. *"Let that mind be in you, which was also in Christ Jesus."* [Phillipians Ch. 2: *vs* 5]

Our own "divided" self can and must be reintegrated in order that we become the living and conscious expression of the Universal Spirit we call God.

The idea that we are separate from one another or separate from the Creator - from LIFE itself! - is a dangerous illusion too long enjoyed by humanity. The cure for all the troubles in our world, and our personal lives, lies within us, in our own true nature.

We humans differ from all the other creatures here because of one <u>Divine</u> aspect of our being, our imagination - our ability to "image in" that which does not yet exist in the outer world. That is precisely why we are said to be "made in the image and likeness of God".

As the famous mystic and philosopher, "Mister" Fred Rogers, informed my child and I one morning, in that soft and profoundly gentle "Mister Rogers" voice: "<u>Everything</u> you see in the world began as an idea in someone's mind. And *your* ideas are just as important, and just as strong."

Amen, brother.

Thus was the entire physical Universe first created by the Great Mind we call God. The Omnipresent Spirit, if you will. That which Einstein *knew* intuitively was there - was everywhere! - could probably "see" it, in his higher mind, but could not quite find the words. We have all experienced things we just could not find words to accurately describe.

This is the time of the reconciling of Creation with the Creator. The time of the awakening of all who are willing to embrace a new awareness, a new identity of themselves as essentially <u>spiritual</u> beings; to *be* the Sons and Daughters of the Most High – the physical embodiments of the Light Itself.

The Reverend William Dove became "Paul Solomon" not by changing his name, but by changing everything he knew about himself as a person. Rest assured it did not happen overnight. It was a long and often arduous process as the "old" man died and the "new" spiritual man was painstakingly born. And so it is for us all. We may be "renewed in the spirit of our minds" in an instant, but our bodies and habits will not disappear without effort and struggle. It takes daily, often moment by moment, acts of a spiritualized will to accomplish – and only we determine just how transformative that Creative Spirit can or will be in our lives.

One question was asked of the Source that is of the utmost importance to share with humanity, especially given what we already know about the apostle Paul as the author of so much of the New Testament.

Once, when explaining the dissolution of his own marriage, Paul described his 'Reverend Bill Dove' self to me: "I was a genuine, macho, buckle-of-the-Bible-Belt, Southern Baptist Minister of the Gospel of Jesus Christ, and proud of it, kind of a John Wayne in a cleric's collar." And as such, he had very serious concerns (especially in the beginning) about exactly what it was that was happening to him.

So he challenged the Voice of the readings the only way he knew - by asking "them" to give testimony about what he knew to be "God's Word", the Holy Bible. Not even Satan would dare lie about the Bible! The question was asked in good old everyday Southern Baptist style:

Conductor: *"Is the Bible as we now have it actually the verbally inspired, faithfully reproduced, and infallible Word of God?"*

The Answer: *"Inherent in this question you ask are actually several questions. First of all, we would correct your wording in this manner: "The 'Word of God' is <u>not</u> written on paper!*

"It is written: 'The Word became flesh, and dwelt among us.' There, then, is the inspired, infallible Word of God. His name was Christ, and that ye have is a record of Him, of His life, of those things of Him which were from the beginning, and those things of His apostles who walked upon this plane. The Bible you take into your hands to read, then, immediately becomes verbally inspired and infallible <u>as you open your heart to God and read through His eyes</u>!

"It is not, then, the book that you read - but He who lives in your heart, that is infallible."

The Book can be an infallible guide, but only if read with the eyes of our Souls. If we use the Bible merely to enhance our own "doubtful disputations", as Paul described the arguments among even the earliest Christians, then that is all we will see.

And that illuminates the most important and immutable law of the universe under which we all labor, without fail: <u>You *will* find what you are looking for</u>. We all do. That is why we are exhorted to "seek first the Kingdom of God", and "keep your eye single". It does not matter whether you love something or hate it, desire it or fear it - that which occupies your mind will manifest in your life, guaranteed!

There is a mechanism described at length in a later reading describing how our thoughts take actual form, made of photons of Light in the higher levels of the mind, and are thus 'magnetized' to us, their creators:

". . . *human beings, have the capacity to use this Force, which is the force of creation itself. This Force is sufficient to literally create a stellar body!*

Attempt to understand in this manner the nature of this Force: You have about you energies which are called particles, sub-atomic particles. These are, in reality, nothing more than polarized vibration. They are not 'substance' at all, but are the foundations, the roots. They are positive, negative and neutral results of charged photons. We use the term photon here to describe a quanta of light having no positive, negative or neutral electrical charge.

This light going forth from the center of the universe, the heart of God, is God Himself existing in all space, time and matter - and outside the constrictions of space, time, and matter. This light, expressed in the form of an indiscrete unit called a photon, has no charge, but is capable of taking on charge. You are surrounded by and filled with these quanta of light. You are full of Light, and Light is what there is. Light is all there is! This is the supreme vibration that is superior to every other expression of life. It is the foundation for vibration, which is second in omniscience and omnipotence to the light which responds to creative thought - for it is the activity and the nature of the brain to release electrical discharge with every thought.

Photons, then, are readily available to be changed in form, to take on "thought form". Thought forms - photons into atoms providing positive, negative and neutral charge - these atomic structures then can be beamed, as it were, or directed by a disciplined mind, toward any distant object. And, in the hands of one so trained, can even penetrate that object.

There is no substance on earth, in earth, in the structure of earth, which can resist penetration by this Force of light set in motion by the creative mind. That is the mind of God expressing through the flesh.

This in turn sets in motion vibration, which becomes the basis of harmony. Harmony, then, through a spectrum of seven basic colors gives birth to a collection of such photons, light, force - and when combined with sound vibration, become a distinct unit. Thus, in such a manner, creation - and life - is completed."

Well, that gives a whole new dimension – indeed, *many* new dimensions – to the concept of taking "personal responsibility". What we "think", is created in thought form – and, thus, it is magnetized to us, and *must* be drawn to us.

Meditation, then, becoming aware of one's own thought processes and beginning to assume control, is our saving grace. It is not so much something one "does", as something one ceases to do – which is to allow random thoughts to capture our attention, becoming energized by our attention to them, and stealing our natural peace and enlightenment.

Psalm 46: verse 10, pretty much says it all: "Be still, and *know* that I AM God" - learning to quiet our mental-chatter so that we might begin to create consciously! This is *the* key to transforming our lives. It is in the practicing of inner stillness that we actually begin to "see" what has always been.

How do we do that? We refocus our awareness. We simply listen until the silence between each thought becomes longer and longer. And as each thought passes by, our "point of reference" then becomes the stillness between the thoughts. Then we begin to see ourselves as the thinker, not the thoughts, and we become aware of our oneness with Life Itself.

From Source: *"Listen. Listen by experiencing the things around you as if they were the very voice of God – speaking directly to you, through what He has put before you!*

Listening to Him, then, becomes a natural part of the life - not something set apart. The messages from the Father come, then, when you are engaged in doing good for another – rather than 'sitting in the silence', as you call it.

"Your perception of the Presence of God will come, then, through the <u>participating with Him,</u> in the living of your life."

Paul Solomon knew he would not be here in the body very long, and often spoke of the short time he was to spend (though he did manage to outlive many of his more dire predictions). But, he could not abide for the same reason Jesus Himself could not be here forever in the flesh. Simply put, it is each individual's *personal* responsibility to learn to know that Presence, the God who lives within. Collectively, it is <u>our</u> time to accept the challenge to "overcome the world" and learn to discern the voice of God amidst the incessant babble that fills most lives. It is time for us all to know, and <u>become,</u> the Living Light! That "Light which lighteth everyone who cometh into the world." Time to take to heart, the words: "Ye are the Light of the world!"

Well, exactly how are we to do this? The same way Yeshua/Jesus did it: By bringing our individual bodies and minds under subjection to Spirit. The individual Soul, returning to its Source by an act of personal will. Paradoxically enough, that happens not by exercising our will, but by actually surrendering our "individual" will, to Love Itself. Believe it, God *is* Love.

In the words of the Source, from one of the very earliest readings:

The purpose here is that there might be those who can understand and teach how this Earth, these bodies, can be brought under subjection. For thou art living in the last days. Know that this generation shall not pass before the Son of God Himself comes in the clouds.

The Christ will walk again upon this Earth, even as He walked in those days in Galilee. He will bring this Earth under subjection and cause it to be the footstool of God Himself. It is for this purpose that these disciplines are given.

You have the opportunity to learn to subject the body to the Soul of man. Study those disciplines of Inner Light Consciousness, as well as bio-feedback methods, and all therapies that teach controlling the body. Learn to use your dreams. Recognize the voice from within, the Spirit of God who walks so heavily in the Earth this day.

It is important that all learn to discern those things of Spirit from the things of the flesh. And how else can such things be discerned, except from within?

Then how would you learn such communication? The teaching given by Him who was the Master of Masters was, "Be still, and know." As you wait often for His voice, there will come the day when His voice will be clearly heard, and will be easily distinguishable from the others.

Jesus said, "Where I go, you know, and the way." What he meant was that there really is only "one way" – inward, to The Source of Life. He could demonstrate the path, but we would have to follow on it. He did all that could be done *for* us. But no one can do for us what we alone must do.

He will meet us in the Holy of Holies, the deepest spaces of our hearts, the highest realms of our souls.

The Christ of God knew, because of His own human experience as the man Jesus/Yeshua, as Paul also knew, that we have an awful habit of following leaders and teachers outside of ourselves. But, because they are outside of us and we can ask *them* how to live our own lives, we cannot grow to our own Divine Destiny. That problem is also the first Commandment: "I AM the lord, thy God, and thou shalt have no false Gods before me." The Living Light within, the true Self, the one and only I AM, is the only revealer of Truth.

A significant danger inherent in any option is also that the world is filled with those who are more than glad to tell you what you should do with your own mind, body, soul and money, so the only real safeguard *is* to learn inner discernment. We can begin with: "By their fruits ye shall know them." Many are they who actually mean well - but, unfortunately, just don't <u>know</u> what it is they seem so sure about. (See: Chapter One!)

More to the point: I once had a dream that made me want to laugh and cry at the same time. Through my experiences conducting Paul's readings I learned that we all want to know the same things, with precious few variations: "Who am I, really?" "Why is my life like this, and what can I do about it?" And, the BIG one: "What am I really here to do?"

In my vision-like dream it seems that the Christ had returned in the flesh, and there was a joyous crowd around Him calling for his attention. It didn't take long to see why enlightenment has to be an inside job. All the people gathered around Him vying for His attention were asking: "Lord, am I saying my prayers right?"; "Is my posture correct when I meditate?"; "Should I be a vegetarian"; "Does my aura look OK?"; "Does this make me look fat?"

OK, not the last one – but, obviously it was a circus.

Believe me, nothing you will ever learn from any other human being (whether friend or psychic-advisor), or watch on a DVD; *or read here*, can begin to convey what happens when you establish communication with the Spirit within you. And the big joke on us all is, nothing *outside* will ever be the same!

Normally, we believe that by changing our outer circumstances we have somehow changed our selves, but we do not change just by changing outer circumstances. It's a spiritual truth: "No matter where you go, there you are." That being said, changing outside circumstances definitely can *initiate* change, but, it's always entirely up to us to "Stay true to the new!" when we are in the midst of being reborn for any reason.

Daily life is the place where the little things seem to ensnare us by keeping us busy. In our current culture, everyday life often resembles some insane cosmic "Whack-a-Mole." But, every circumstance and situation exists for a reason. And that is, simply to awaken us to our true nature. Every "problem" is merely an opportunity to manifest our divine nature. It's a "problem" only when we are seeing it from the purely physical point of view, and insist on solving it by just manipulating matter, not learning from it.

It has been said: The first step toward getting out of a hole is to stop digging. Here's a mantra you may use anytime, but especially when a situation begins to appear overwhelming or unsolvable. Just stop and ask yourself: *"If this was a dream, what would it mean?"*

In other words: What am I trying to teach me, about me...

Yes, in the search for the true Self, there is plenty of time for "me".

When we begin to look at daily situations as the machinations of our own Soul, situations created specifically by and for us to confront, decipher the message therein, and make corrections, Life becomes an entirely new game. One in which we are no longer at the mercy of events. The most important teaching shared in the ILC Course is the understanding of our individual lives as custom-made (designed before we entered!) "Mystery Schools", and that our daily life experiences are specifically created by us to provide situations that will *require* us to access our divine nature in order to heal them, and awaken.

There is absolutely no other reason for anything that happens to us. We are experiencing something we have either long ago caused, or something we have volunteered to experience (even if we don't 'deserve' it) in order to heal and raise ourselves and the world around us. That is what the Christ did, as Jesus/Yeshua; and that is what the Christ now does through us, as us. Our day-to-day lives now become part of The Great Passion Play, written on what the Source called "the skein of Time & Space."

Each one of our own unique Cosmic Dramas is being very personally, and very physically, played out in the third dimension – on a planet that has already been described as "a stage" by one of the master play-writes of all time.

Once you decide to become aware of and accept that premise, everything immediately gets better. And, you do not have to join a new religion or adopt any new philosophical system – unless, of course, you already have one that does *not* solve your problems. You'll want to get rid of that anyway!

Each circumstance being different for every soul, the healing of any specific situation will require a solution for one person that someone else can't even imagine. However, the non-specific guaranteed-to-work-every-time cure for whatever ails us is always - commit some act of _divine_ Love. Some giving of self without thought of return, an act that entails approaching another person or situation – or even ourselves - in ways we have neglected until now. Now we can do it for the best reason of all: It needs to be done - - and besides, nothing else has worked.

A New and Larger Perspective of "I"

Simultaneously, our lives are lived not just on this planet but in a Solar System, a Solar System that is also part of a galaxy careening through an expanding Universe. Each of the planets in this system provides experiences for us on various specific levels of vibration. We already understand the different levels of Light of our "visible" spectrum: violet, indigo, blue, green, yellow, orange, and red. (That is not their actual order. The nuns who taught me in grades 1 thru 8 all agreed that VIBGYOR [pronounced: Vib-gee-yore] would be easier to remember than IVBGYOR). They are merely the levels of light energy which the human eye is able to perceive. But, we are now aware of infra-red; ultra-violet; X-ray; etc., literally, *ad infinitum.*

What most of us are not consciously aware of (though there are many who are) is that we exist - and have "bodies" - on all these different levels of light. Our higher-level bodies have less and less definition or form, as we move upward in rate of vibration, becoming less dense in our expression.

Still, an Edgar Cayce reading said it perfectly and it should be meditated upon long and often by any who would come to know the Truth: "*Yea, though there be planets, other systems, galaxies, even Universes! The Soul of man – thine own Soul! – encompasses all of these!*"

Ponder that, "...thine own Soul, encompasses all of these"! Now *that* is a state of mind, and heart, to aspire to. Of course, we need to truly <u>know</u> it.

God's Truth: I once spent some dream-time on the Moon with Archangel Michael [really!]. I felt quite "awake" and lucid, and very physical. I even kicked the silvery-grey dust at my feet to see if it would rise and scatter - it did! Like fine grey sand or powder, in slow motion, and slowly floated back down.

Michael had a very human-like body (no wings) and was attired in an impeccably tailored silver one-button suit, with a shining white shirt reflecting the pure sunlight, and a perfectly knotted silver tie that perfectly complimented his perfectly tailored suit.

Exquisite!

Except that his face would not settle into a stable configuration - it was a human face, but it appeared to be made of mercury or liquid light, and would not stay in a distinct set of features.

But, I knew *exactly* who he was!

As we were looking into each other's eyes, I detected motion peripherally off to my right. A few hundred feet away a huge, angry and malevolent frog-like creature climbed out of a crater. It had long sharp teeth and gave the very real and menacing impression that I was its quarry. As it leaped toward us in great bounds in the low gravity, Archangel Michael slowly pulled a chrome-plated .45 automatic (just like the one I had carried in the Air Force, but obviously much cooler!) and shot it once, the weapon recoiling in his hand and arm, the shell casing flying out of it and landing in the dust a good way from us, but making no sound in the airless environment, the bullet striking the beast and causing it to fall and then slowly disappear. I was shocked and telepathically (with a touch of surprise and righteous indignation!) said, "But I thought we are not supposed to kill!?"

Looking deeply into my soul, he said softly - "Some things have to die. These are your creation, and only you can - and must - kill them." Then he too slowly disappeared. Leaving me standing alone in the bright sunlight.

My personal understanding of the Moon was that it represented our subconscious, which meant that he was telling me, in the symbols of our little vignette, that the "monsters" within us (our fears, anger, hatreds we might harbor unconsciously, feelings that we might even feel justified in harboring, or believe we have already left behind because they are out of harmony with Divine Love) are still our responsibility, alone. No one can heal what is within us but ourselves, and that is the *only* way they will be cleansed from our psyches. It must be an act of conscious volition. They were created by our individual wills and fears, and only we can make them go away – but, only by being a much higher part of ourselves than we are accustomed to.

Life will present us with the opportunities to conquer those things. We must recognize them as such, and in that moment we can truly conquer our inner demons. Still, we often do this while blissfully unaware that this is what we are doing, and it does happen virtually every day of our lives!

Once, during a "work" reading for the early Fellowship, the Source congratulated those of us gathered for having "passed through an initiation" successfully. We looked around at each other quizzically, shrugging our shoulders while trying to determine what might have transpired amongst us to elicit such a comment. Sensing our confusion, the Source explained to us that in the course of our daily lives situations occur which may cause us to feel angry and resentful, even with those we love. When that happens, and we choose *not* to respond in the old ways – but, instead *choose* to use our newfound commitment to *being* love and seeking understanding - in that moment we are raised and are lifted into the Light! And, we have brought that same Light into the world! We have dispelled darkness by changing our minds and taking command of our feelings – and we have lifted others as well.

We had all been permanently changed, and brought the whole human race closer to the Godhead - through a conscious act of personal will, in harmony with the will of the Highest Within us! Needless to say, that moment changed the nature of our everyday lives forever.

Finally

Our true self is literally made of Light: "...in the Image and likeness of God."

The logical/rational mind can take great peace from embracing that, and understanding this simple statement: "You don't *have* a Soul, you <u>are</u> a Soul. What you *have* is an identity problem."

It doesn't matter who said it, it's just true – and, obviously, unbelievably important. Once you begin to truly embrace that concept you will be able, indeed forced, to see yourself as God sees you - in all your true glory! (And, <u>everyone</u> else, too. And there's the rub.)

All of the attributes of our Souls, everything we believe and hope we will be someday "up in heaven", become immediately available! Right here. Right now. It is all within us, and always has been!

To be sure, there is much work to be done, but even the smallest efforts in our life have enormous consequences for us and everyone we touch. It's the only job we have: To truly be, <u>*all*</u> that we can be.

Not to be consciously aware of one's true Self is, in the words of an old *Hindu* allegory, to be like a fish swimming around wondering if there really is such a thing as water.

If that image resonates within you, and you would like some sound advice and guidance, you can enhance your personal search for The Source of All Life by accessing the work of our good friend Paul, at *The Paul Solomon Foundation* website:

www.PaulSolomon.com

There you will find not just his story, but your own. Along with some guidance that will assist you in finding your way within, from the many readings already transcribed for publication.

I will end with a few reading excerpts that I hope might change the way you see life, your own and everyone else's. And *do* avail yourself of two books Paul and I both read long before we met. They helped guide us both, and millions of others:

"The Impersonal Life" and *"Christ in you."*

You will be glad you did.

We will begin with a reading given in Japan for a young woman. It describes our own creation in the heart of God, and the experiences that began our 'self' awareness, which must, sooner or later, culminate in remembering our origin - our original "Self" realization. I will include the entirety of the reading as the description of her problems and the desire for healing and direction mirror the thoughts and needs of all of us. The Source was adamant that these readings were not given for anyone alone, but for us all.

Please, *please,* read this as if it is you that is being described - because it is. It was all of us, there, in the beginning when we sprang forth from The Sea of Love and Light that we call God, Creator, Great Spirit, Source, The One, I AM.

Paul Solomon Reading 9529 Japan / April 25, 1992

You will have before you the records and enquiring mind of ...(Name)... born ... in ...You will give relationships to universal forces and comment on purpose and personality, past and present, latent and manifest. You will answer the questions I now ask.

Q. In the future, will I get an encounter with a man whom I'll be attracted to? As a woman I want to have an experience of giving birth to a baby and raising one. Will my dream come true?

A. Yes, ... (Name)... yes we have the soul records here: The movement of the soul through progressive times of growth, incarnation, bonding and awakening to realizations in soul growth.

Now let us take these questions in just a bit of a different order that we may establish the manner, means of growth to this point, to discover why the soul has entered into this country, this family under these circumstances, and having so established we will then return to the initial question.

This is a soul who was born into self-awareness through the activities of the school called by the ancient manner the Temple Beautiful. Now the awakening of a soul to self-awareness refers to the time when this soul first experienced being separated in consciousness from that great single soul which is the expression of God; God's One Child.[The Christ, The Word, The Solar Logos, etc.] *And, yet, this One Child, this singular expression of God, is something you might view, taking from the Master of Masters and the scribes of the Bible, taking their own analogy we would use it here in this manner to say that perhaps you could think of God's One Child, who is characterized by Love, Life and the Light of Enlightenment – and, to the extent that these energies exist, they exist as the very nature, character, of God's One Child - and using the ancient rabbinical analogy, you might see this One Child as if it were a desert, or seashore with so many billions of grains of sand.*

Now we use that analogy, that metaphor, because it was used by the Ancients, particularly in speaking to Abraham: that his lineage would be as the number of grains of sand within a desert or seashore. Thus, if you consider the desert One, and the multitude of cells or expressions within that One, then there is originally, in soul consciousness, a relationship only with the One desert itself as One whole, and there is no consciousness at all of a grain of sand within that great body being a singular expression. No grain of sand upon this great shore could think of itself as anything but the shore itself, never self-awareness, until the soul is allowed by the Manu - a word which means literally the "elder brothers" (we would point as well that the Manu also are the Lords of Karma.) Thus, according to the direction of the Manu, the Elohim, these expressions within this Child of God are allowed to have the experience of moving away from the One great singular body to project itself into matter for the purpose of becoming eventually both self-aware, and aware of self only as an expression of the One singular whole.

Then as souls are called from this One great body of the Child of God, called by the Manu into the opportunity for expression, then at that time the soul has its first glimpse of the Earth, not only as one portion of the whole, not just as another grain of sand in the great body, but the soul begins to see the separation between the grains of sand and begins to see the spectacular image of the Universe, the glittering and most awe inspiring experience that one could behold. And the soul, even then, has quite a strain to gain any sense of the enormity, the complexity, the incredible beauty and wonder of this creation of God. But the soul is called aside from the great body for the purpose of allowing that soul to participate in co-creation with God, because creation is not nearly complete. This is the chosen Seventh Day in which the One Child, within whom are the multitude of children of God - and it is the decision, the mandate of the great Creator that each facet of His Being shall work <u>with</u> Him in exploring and discovering all possible concepts, all possible structures, all possible expressions of creation, which might under any circumstances, exist.

And this One great Creator of whom all the sands of the seashore, all the stars of the heavens are a part of that body, this body, this Creator, does not recognize at all the relationships which individuals on this planet have chosen to refer to as Good and Evil. The Creator, Source, is only interested in the myriad expressions of which His children are capable, including those that from the perspective of an individual on this planet might be seen as loathsome, evil, destructive and such, these are seen by the Source as the growing process of souls exploring all their possibilities, and in their maturity making decisions as to what is not in the best interest of higher creation. And in such a manner the Father, the Source, sees only the growth of His children, throughout eternity.

Now with that concept in place, we will refer again to the fact that this particular soul, called out of the great mass to experience self-awareness, first beheld the Earth and influenced activities on the Earth along with the hosts of Elohim continuing creation on Earth. This activity was without a sense of separation. Then, as many other souls have chosen to do, this soul made a choice to project itself into a *physical form, material matter - the result of creative action - but which in itself is <u>alive</u> and always active.*

Now when a soul enters into such a body, a vehicle, the sensory faculties of that animal-form become [the] primary means of gaining information, whereas before the experience in the body, the information came and appeared as realizations, without use of senses.

Thus the soul began to explore sensory experience of different types, at least five different experiences of the environment, which were opportunities of the soul to experience other facets of creation. And in the use of those senses and the experience of the appetites, there is such a need of the occupying soul to manage such a body and process information coming in through the five senses, that in almost every instance the higher senses fade into the background, appearing only as influences, ideas: not discriminatory, not clear, and not easily accessed above the brain's busy processing of information through the five senses.

Now, in that manner a soul becomes captured or imprisoned within a beast. And it becomes then the work of the elder brethren, those who have been through this experience before, and have awakened again to higher consciousness, it becomes their work to take such beasts and expose them to stimuli that will remind the consciousness within the beast that there is a Divine Order: That there is an expression of the Divine, that there is an indwelling presence that is, in fact, the true intrinsic soul itself.

But this soul within the beast lies completely dormant in terms of activity or influence, because it has entered the beast only as an observer, to observe and see and learn of the functions, the activities, the experiences which are possible upon this plane, this school, this Earth.

This Observer Self is the one and only true Intrinsic Self; it is the soul itself, it is the identity; it does not change from one experience to another, one lifetime to another. It is one and the same, it has always existed, and always will; it is incapable of experiencing death.

And this Observer Self, this witness gathering the experience, exploring the nature of creation, will not assert itself within the beast except in certain important circumstances. Sometimes, though not always, this Observer Self, Intrinsic Self, the real and true self, may intervene in survival threatening situations relating to the beast. More often, the soul, the Intrinsic Self, responds to any expression of the divine expression of the heart of God that manifests within its presence.

And such expressions include music as harmony and attunement; such expressions include beauty in the myriad forms in which it occurs. Such expressions are spoken of by the Apostle Paul in his writing of the epistle to the Romans: in the first chapter in which he refers to so many expressions of life, so many expressions of God in the environment around every soul, that it leaves any particular soul without an excuse for failing to recognize, and respond to, and join with this omnipresent expression of God.

Now in the case of this soul who sits before us, we see the Manu accepting this soul for building its awareness, for recalling, for sharing the awareness of the Intrinsic Self with the rest of the body, so that the entire being becomes aware of itself as an expression of God.

The Manu have chosen three Temples for this purpose, one of those being that school or place called the Temple Beautiful, in which the embodied soul is exposed to music, to rhythm, colors, dimension, texture, design, all forms of beauty. And in this practice of exposing the beast to myriad forms of beauty there is an awakening in the soul, there is a response from the non-assertive Intrinsic Self, a response of excitement, of recognition, of desire to participate in the creation of such beauty. And this is the awakening of the soul to self-awareness or self-consciousness.

Therefore as the Manu of the Temples saw a body, or a beast, responding with delight to rhythms, beginning to participate in producing sound and beauty, as the beast might begin an attempt to sing with the Music of the Spheres in participation, then the Manu declare that the soul is now ready for its journey through incarnation experience, to gather many opportunities to exercise, to use that Intrinsic Self for the just and right purposeful causes of eliminating all disharmony on this planet and transforming it to an expression of love and of God. Thus this soul was awakened.

In time you learned about mantra, and of what can be called chanting: the repetition of rhythmic sounds designed to dis-inhibit the cerebral cortex. So "thinking," in terms that you understand thinking - that which occurs in the cerebral cortex - this is then dis-inhibited or rendered inactive by the chanting of rhythmic sounds. And when the cerebral cortex is so dis-inhibited there is the ability of the body to fall into a trance-like state, which allows the Intrinsic Self or the Higher Self to manifest more effectively throughout the body, and to heighten spiritual evolution and bring the body, the consciousness, ever closer to God. Now this experience of chanting and such, you might find both in India and in the Shinto chanting of Japan, particularly the ancient Ko-Shinto who understood the magic vibrations of such sound.

This brings you then to the present life and your questions about it. You are participating in an activity that is a good use of your soul in its past experiences. We will ask you here to particularly think of those moments when you sing, when you are performing your jazz improvisations, the moments when you feel almost as if the music has taken over and is expressing itself through you rather than having the experience of yourself attempting to control or produce the music.

As you recall those moments when the music sings itself, these are the moments when the Intrinsic Self, the real you, the true Self, is expressing itself through the body. These are the moments in which you are closest to the Divine Presence, when you have called the Master of Masters into the environment.

And in such moments, those exposed to your music cannot resist opening the heart and awakening their own Intrinsic Self, and be lifted a little closer to the <u>experience</u> of God.

A final word, from the Heart of God:

Paul Solomon Reading 1069

"There is no substitute, and never will be, for attuning within yourself to the Source of self. There is too great a willingness among you to depend upon others for guidance, thus giving up the responsibility within yourself for discovering Truth. There is no way to substitute your own responsibility for knowing the Source of self that is ever and always within you.

You will only recognize the harmony in another's words, and in their teachings, by developing that ability to listen within to harmony within the Source of yourself. Through turning within, through meditation, through taking responsibility for making discoveries within the self, rather than fanciful entertainments with images and ideas and the worship of a guru or a teacher, or such.

Go beyond that to the discovery of information within yourself, and then when you hear, recognize, feel that harmony of another speaking from that Source, so the Spirit within you will recognize the Spirit in that one. You build, then, cooperation and support for that you recognize. No substitute for that recognition.

But recognition comes only when you separate those impulses of the senses, and the appetites, the appeal to ego, the appeal to drama, and such.

Look, rather, for that within you that makes a demand upon you that you order your life and your thoughts, with those about.

That Force within you that causes an impulse to <u>love</u>, and <u>accept,</u> and <u>support</u>; that impulse within you that causes Love, without requirement on others that they change, or meet your expectations or belief system.

That within you that gives an ability to discover an element which can be loved in the heart of others, however dark their actions.

Remember: *"God is not living in us, or even through us. God is living as us."*

So be it...

Acknowledgement

I would like to acknowledge the great help and inspiration of those who have contributed, each in their own unique way, to bring this work to fruition. In alphabetical order, but certainly not in order of consequence or importance:

Nanette Crist, Doris herself, Christian van Hoose (*"How's the book comin' Dad?"*), Sandra van Hoose (*"Where's your book!!!?"*), and Rob Whitehead.

And, of course, those on both sides of "the veil" who have made me who I AM - especially, Edgar, Paul, and all who serve the One so selflessly.

Also, the great artist and poet, Paul Simon, for: *"We come and we go. It's a thing that I keep in the back of my head..."*

Thank you, all of you, from the very heights of my Soul to the depths of my Heart, for all your love, kindness and honesty.

Michael W. McCarthy